lonely planet

ROUTE 66

- - - - - - - - - - - - - - -

ROAD TRIPS

This edition written and researched by

Karla Zimmerman, Amy Balfour & Nate Cavalieri

HOW TO USE THIS BOOK

Reviews

In the Destinations section:

All reviews are ordered in our authors' preference, starting with their most preferred option. Additionally:

Sights are arranged in the geographic order that we suggest you visit them and, within this order, by author preference.

Eating and Sleeping reviews are ordered by price range (budget, midrange, top end) and, within these ranges, by author preference.

Map Legend

Routes

	Trip Route
	Trip Detour
	Linked Trip
	Walk Route
	Tollway
	Freeway
	Primary
	Secondary
	Tertiary
	Lane
	Unsealed Road
	Plaza/Mall
	Steps
	Tunnel
	Pedestrian Overpass
	Walk Track/Path

Boundaries

	International
	State/Province
	Cliff

Population

✪	Capital (National)
◉	Capital (State/Province)
●	City/Large Town
●	Town/Village

Transport

✈	Airport
	Cable Car/ Funicular
	Parking
	Train/Railway
	Tram
Ⓜ	Underground Train Station

Trips

1	Trip Numbers
9	Trip Stop
	Walking Tour
	Trip Detour

Highway Route Markers

97	US National Hwy
5	US Interstate Hwy
44	California State Hwy

Hydrography

	River/Creek
	Intermittent River
	Swamp/Mangrove
	Canal
	Water
	Dry/Salt/ Intermittent Lake
	Glacier

Areas

	Beach
	Cemetery (Christian)
	Cemetery (Other)
	Park
	Forest
	Reservation
	Urban Area
	Sportsground

Symbols In This Book

✔	Top Tips	🍴	Food & Drink
🔗	Link Your Trips	🌳	Outdoors
💡	Tips from Locals	📷	Essential Photo
➡	Trip Detour	🏃	Walking Tour
📖	History & Culture	🍴	Eating
👪	Family	🛏	Sleeping

⊙	Sights	🛏	Sleeping
🏊	Beaches	🍴	Eating
🏃	Activities	🍷	Drinking
🎓	Courses	☆	Entertainment
👉	Tours	🛍	Shopping
✻	Festivals & Events	ℹ	Information & Transport

These symbols and abbreviations give vital information for each listing:

☎	Telephone number	🐾	Pet-friendly
☺	Opening hours	🚌	Bus
P	Parking	⛴	Ferry
⊖	Nonsmoking	🚋	Tram
❄	Air-conditioning	🚆	Train
@	Internet access	apt	apartments
🛜	Wi-fi access	d	double rooms
🏊	Swimming pool	dm	dorm beds
🌱	Vegetarian selection	q	quad rooms
		r	rooms
🍴	English-language menu	s	single rooms
		ste	suites
👪	Family-friendly	tr	triple rooms
		tw	twin rooms

CONTENTS

PLAN YOUR TRIP

Welcome to Route 66 5

Route 66 Map 6

Route 66 Highlights 8

Chicago City Guide 10

Los Angeles City Guide 11

Need to Know 12

ROAD TRIPS

1 Eastern
Route 66   5–7 Days 17

2 Central
Route 66   5–7 Days 27

3 Western
Route 66   3–4 Days 39

DESTINATIONS

Eastern Route 66 50

Illinois... 50

Chicago... 50

Springfield 59

Missouri.. 60

St Louis... 60

Kansas... 65

Oklahoma 65

Tulsa 65

Oklahoma City 67

Central Route 66 70

Texas...70

New Mexico 70

Albuquerque 73

Santa Fe..79

Gallup 89

Arizona.. 90

Petrified Forest National Park 90

Holbrook & Around.........................91

Winslow 91

Walnut Canyon
National Monument...................... 92

Flagstaff... 92

Kingman...97

Topock Gorge to Oatman............. 99

Western Route 66 100

Los Angeles 100

Barstow 108

USA DRIVING GUIDE

USA DRIVING GUIDE 111

Motorcyclists on Route 66, California

WEST

SAN BERNARDINO
66
COUNTY

WELCOME TO
ROUTE 66

For a classic American road trip, nothing beats good ol' Route 66. Nicknamed the nation's 'Mother Road' by novelist John Steinbeck, this string of small-town main streets and country byways first connected big-shouldered Chicago with the waving palm trees of Los Angeles in 1926.

Whether you seek to explore retro Americana or simply want to experience big horizons and captivating scenery far from the madding crowd, Route 66 will take you there. Mingle with farmers in Illinois and country-and-western stars in Missouri; hear the legends of cowboys and Indians in Oklahoma; visit Native American tribal nations and contemporary pueblos across the Southwest, all the while discovering the traditions of the USA's indigenous peoples. Then follow the trails of miners and desperados deep into the Old West. At road's end lie the Pacific beaches of sun-kissed Southern California.

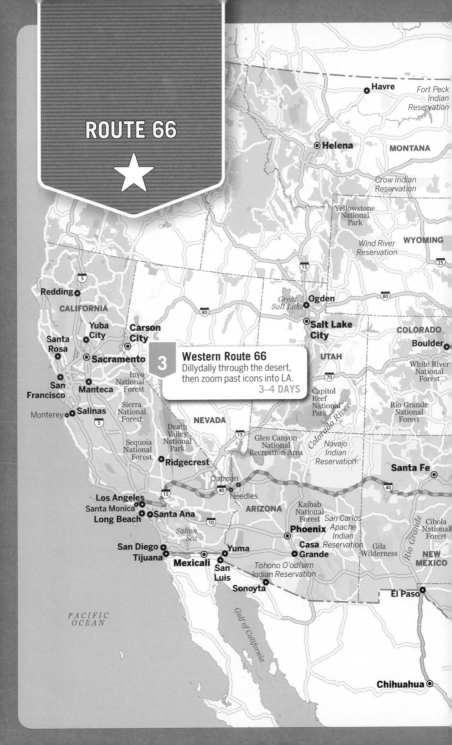

ROUTE 66

⭐

3 Western Route 66
Dillydally through the desert, then zoom past icons into LA.
3–4 DAYS

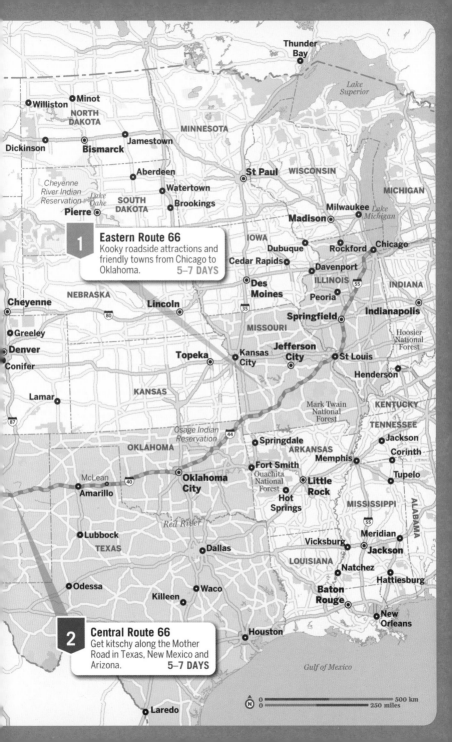

1 Eastern Route 66
Kooky roadside attractions and friendly towns from Chicago to Oklahoma. **5–7 DAYS**

2 Central Route 66
Get kitschy along the Mother Road in Texas, New Mexico and Arizona. **5–7 DAYS**

Thunder Bay

Lake Superior

Williston • Minot
NORTH DAKOTA
Dickinson
Bismarck • Jamestown

MINNESOTA

Aberdeen
St Paul **WISCONSIN**
Lake Oahe • Watertown **MICHIGAN**
Pierre **SOUTH DAKOTA** • Brookings
Madison Milwaukee *Lake Michigan*
Rockford Chicago
IOWA
Dubuque
Cedar Rapids • Davenport
Des Moines **ILLINOIS** [55]
NEBRASKA Peoria **INDIANA**
Lincoln
Springfield Indianapolis
Cheyenne [80] **MISSOURI**
Hoosier National Forest
Greeley
Denver Topeka Kansas City Jefferson City St Louis
Conifer
Henderson
Lamar **KANSAS** **KENTUCKY**
[87]
Mark Twain National Forest **TENNESSEE**
Osage Indian Reservation [44] Springdale • Jackson
OKLAHOMA **ARKANSAS** Corinth
Fort Smith Memphis
McLean [40] Oklahoma City *Ouachita National Forest* Little Rock Tupelo
Amarillo Hot Springs
Red River **MISSISSIPPI**
Lubbock
TEXAS Meridian
Dallas Vicksburg Jackson
LOUISIANA
Odessa Waco Natchez
Killeen Hattiesburg
Baton Rouge
Houston New Orleans

Gulf of Mexico

Laredo

Cheyenne River Indian Reservation

ALABAMA
[55]

N 0 ————— 500 km
0 ————— 250 miles

ROUTE 66
HIGHLIGHTS

★

Tucumcari (above) Home to one of the best-preserved sections of Route 66, including dozens of neon signs that cast a rainbow-colored glow. See it on Trip 2

Munger Moss Motel, Lebanon (right) This atmospheric motel has welcomed passing travelers for over 40 years. See it on Trip 1

Santa Monica (left) The end of the line: 2400 miles from its start in Chicago, Route 66 comes to an end in the Los Angeles beachside suburb. See it on Trip 3

CITY GUIDE

Downtown Chicago

CHICAGO

The Windy City will blow you away with its cloud-scraping architecture and lakefront beaches. High and low culture comfortably coexist without any taint of pretension. Take in world-class museums and landmark theater stages, or drop by divey blues clubs and graffiti-scrawled pizzerias – they're all equally beloved in 'Chi-town'.

Getting Around

Driving Chicago's well-laid-out street grid is slow, but not too difficult, except around the Loop. If you're exploring downtown and other neighborhoods served by 'El' lines, ditch your car for the day and get around on foot and by train (or bus) instead.

Parking

Overnight hotel parking and city parking garages are expensive. Metered on-street parking is easier to find in outlying neighborhoods than around downtown, but it's not necessarily cheap (occasionally it's free in residential areas).

Where to Eat

Essential eats include Chicago-style hot dogs, Italian beef sandwiches and deep-dish pizza. Star chefs run restaurants in the West Loop and on the North Side. For an eclectic mix of cafes, bistros, gastropubs and more, nose around Wicker Park, Bucktown and Andersonville.

Where to Stay

Base yourself in the Loop for convenient 'El' train stops, seek luxury on the Gold Coast or look for deals at the Near North's boutique and high-rise hotels. For more personalized stays, book a B&B in a trendy neighborhood such as Wicker Park.

Useful Websites

Choose Chicago (www.choosechicago.com) Official tourist information site.

CTA (www.transitchicago.com) Bus and train maps, schedules and fares.

Chicago Reader (www.chicagoreader.com) Alternative weekly covering events, arts and entertainment.

Road Trip through Chicago: 1
Destinations coverage: p50

Venice Beach, Los Angeles

LOS ANGELES

Loony LA, land of starstruck dreams and Hollywood Tinseltown magic. You may think you know what to expect: celebrity worship, Botoxed beach blondes, endless traffic and earthquakes. But it's also California's most ethnically diverse city, with new immigrants arriving daily, evolving the boundary-breaking global arts, music and food scenes.

Getting Around

Angelenos drive everywhere. Freeway traffic jams are endless, but worst during morning and afternoon rush hours. Metro operates buses and subway and light-rail trains (fares $1.50), with limited night and weekend services. DASH minibuses (single-ride 50¢) zip around downtown; Santa Monica's Big Blue Bus (fares $1) connects West LA. Taxis cost $2.80 per mile; meters start at $2.85.

Parking

Street parking is tough. Meters take coins, sometimes credit cards; central pay stations accept coins or cards. Valet parking is ubiquitous, typically $5 to $10 plus tip. Overnight hotel parking averages $25 to $40.

Where to Eat

Food trucks are a local obsession. Downtown cooks up a worldly mix with Little Tokyo, Chinatown, Thai Town, Koreatown and Latin-flavored East LA nearby. Trend-setting eateries inhabit Hollywood, Mid-City, Santa Monica and Venice.

Where to Stay

For beach life, escape to Santa Monica or Venice. Long Beach is convenient to Disneyland and Orange County. Party people adore Hollywood; culture vultures, Downtown LA.

Useful Websites

LA Inc (http://discover-losangeles.com) City's official tourism website.

LA Weekly (www.laweekly.com) Arts, entertainment, dining and events calendar.

Lonely Planet (www.lonelyplanet.com/usa/los-angeles) Travel tips, hotel reservations and travelers' forums.

Road Trip through Los Angeles: 3
Destinations coverage: p100

NEED ^{TO} KNOW

CELL PHONES

The only foreign phones that will work in the USA are GSM multiband models. Network coverage is often spotty in remote areas (eg mountains, deserts).

INTERNET ACCESS

Wi-fi is available at most coffee shops and lodgings. Some accommodations have free guest computers. Cybercafes ($6 to $12 per hour) are common in cities.

FUEL

Gas stations are everywhere, except in national parks and remote areas. Expect to pay $4 to $5 per US gallon.

RENTAL CARS

Alamo (www.alamo.com)

Car Rental Express (www. carrentalexpress.com)

Simply Hybrid (www. simplyhybrid.com)

Zipcar (www.zipcar.com)

IMPORTANT NUMBERS

American Automobile Association (AAA; ☏877-428-2277)

Emergencies (☏911)

Highway conditions (☏800-427-7623)

Traffic updates (☏511)

Climate

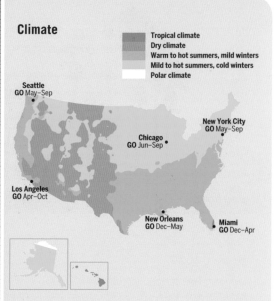

- Tropical climate
- Dry climate
- Warm to hot summers, mild winters
- Mild to hot summers, cold winters
- Polar climate

Seattle GO May–Sep

New York City GO May–Sep

Chicago GO Jun–Sep

Los Angeles GO Apr–Oct

New Orleans GO Dec–May

Miami GO Dec–Apr

When to Go

High Season (Jun–Aug)

» Warm days across the country, with generally high temperatures.

» Busiest season, with big crowds and higher prices.

» In ski resort areas, January to March is high season.

Shoulder Season (Oct & Apr–May)

» Milder temps, fewer crowds.

» Spring flowers (April); fiery autumn colors (October) in many parts.

Low Season (Nov–Mar)

» Wintery days, with snowfall in the north, and heavier rains in some regions.

» Lowest prices for accommodations (aside from ski resorts and warmer getaway destinations).

Daily Costs

Budget: less than $75

» Camping: $20–40

» Meals in roadside diners and cafes: $10–20

» Graze farmers markets for cheaper eats

» Hit the beach and find 'free days' at museums

Midrange: $75–200

» Two-star motel or hotel double room: $75–150

» Meals in casual and midrange restaurants: $20–40

» Theme-park admission: $40–100

Top end: over $200

» Three-star lodging: from $150 per night in high season, more for ocean views

» Three-course meal in top restaurant: $75 plus wine

Eating

Roadside diners & cafes Cheap and simple; abundant only outside cities.

Beach shacks Casual burgers, shakes and seafood meals with ocean views.

National, state & theme parks Mostly so-so, overpriced cafeteria-style or deli picnic fare.

Vegetarians Food restrictions and allergies can usually be catered for at restaurants.

Eating price indicators represent the average cost of a main dish:

$	less than $10
$$	$10–$20
$$$	more than $20

Sleeping

Motels & hotels Ubiquitous along well-trafficked highways and in major tourist areas.

Camping & cabins Ranging from rustic campsites to luxury 'glamping' resorts.

B&Bs Quaint, romantic and pricey inns, found in most coastal and mountain towns.

Hostels Cheap and basic, but almost exclusively in cities.

Price indicators represent the average cost of a double room with private bathroom:

$	less than $100
$$	$100–$200
$$$	more than $200

Arriving in the USA

O'Hare International Airport Chicago

Rental cars Major companies all have outlets at the airport and downtown.

Public transit Blue Line runs to the Loop 24/7 in around 40 minutes; $5.

Shared van service Airport Express to downtown for $32 per person. Vans leave every 15 minutes; journey takes around 60 minutes.

Taxis 30 to 50 minutes to the Loop; around $50.

Los Angeles International Airport

Rental cars Major companies offer shuttles to off-airport lots.

Door-to-door shared-ride shuttles $16 to $25 one way (reservations recommended).

Taxis $30 to $50 plus tip to Santa Monica, Hollywood or Downtown LA; 30 minutes to one hour.

Buses Take Shuttle C (free) to LAX City Bus Center or Metro FlyAway bus ($7) to Downtown LA.

Money

ATMs widely available. Credit cards accepted almost universally.

Tipping

Tipping is expected. Standard tips: 18% to 20% in restaurants; 15% for taxis; $1 per drink in bars; $2 per bag for porters.

Opening Hours

Banks 8:30am–4:30pm Mon–Fri, some to 5:30pm Fri, 9am–12:30pm Sat

Business hours (general) 9am–5pm Mon–Fri

Post offices 9am–5pm Mon–Fri, some 9am–noon Sat

Restaurants 7am–10:30am, 11:30am–2:30pm & 5–9:30pm daily, some later Fri & Sat

Shops 10am–6pm Mon-Sat, noon–5pm Sun (malls open later)

Useful Websites

Lonely Planet (www.lonelyplanet.com/usa/california) Destination info, hotel bookings, travelers' forums and more.

Roadside America (www.roadsideamerica.com) For all things weird and wacky.

For more, see USA Driving Guide (p111)

Road Trips

1 **Eastern Route 66 5–7 Days**
Start your trip in the Windy City, then head south through Kansas and Oklahoma. (p17)

2 **Central Route 66 5–7 Days**
Get kitschy along the Mother Road in Texas, New Mexico and Arizona. (p27)

3 **Western Route 66 3–4 Days**
Dillydally through the desert, then zoom past retro icons into LA. (p39)

Wigwam Motel, Holbrook, Arizona
WALTER BIBIKOW / GETTY IMAGES ©

Eastern Route 66

1

Argue all you want, but we know that 66's goofiest roadside attractions, friendliest small towns and best pie-filled diners pop up on the eastern swath, from Chicago to western Oklahoma.

TRIP HIGHLIGHTS

155 miles

Atlanta
Pie and a hot
dog-loving lumberjack

START
Chicago

3

Springfield

450 miles

Lebanon
Ozark neon, root beer
and bowling

St Louis

7

Tulsa

Clinton

10

FINISH

790 miles

Oklahoma
Route 66 Museum
Multimedia trove tells
the road's story

5–7 DAYS
1050 MILES/
1690KM

GREAT FOR...

BEST TIME TO GO
May–Sep

**ESSENTIAL
PHOTO**

The Gemini Giant, a
fiberglass spaceman,
in Wilmington, IL

**BEST TWO
DAYS**

Oklahoma has
more miles of the
original alignment
than anywhere, plus
cowboys and chicken-
fried steak

Left Gemini Giant, Launching Pad Drive-In (p19)

1 Eastern Route 66

It's a lonely road – a ghost road really – that appears for a stretch then disappears, gobbled up by the interstate. You know you've found it again when a 20ft lumberjack holding a hot dog rises from the side of the road, or a sign points you to the 'World's Largest Covered Wagon,' driven by giant Abe Lincoln. And that's just Illinois! Missouri, Kansas and Oklahoma also waft kitsch aplenty along the route's eastern leg.

❶ Chicago (p50)

Route 66 kicks off in downtown Chicago on Adams St just west of Michigan Ave. Before you snap the obligatory photo with the 'Route 66 Begin' sign (on the south side of Adams), spend some time exploring the Windy City. Wander through the **Art Institute** (📞312-443-3600; www.artic.edu; 111 S Michigan Ave; adult/child $23/free; 🕙10:30am-5pm, to 8pm Thu; ♿; Ⓜ Brown, Orange, Green, Purple, Pink Line to Adams) – steps from the Mother Road's launching point – and browse Edward Hopper's *Nighthawks* (a diner scene) and Grant Wood's *American Gothic* (a farmer portrait) to set the scene for what you'll see en route. Nearby **Millennium Park** (📞312-742-1168; www.millenniumpark.org; 201 E Randolph St; 🕙6am-11pm; ♿; Ⓜ Brown, Orange, Green, Purple, Pink Line to Randolph) is just plain cool, with mod public artworks and concerts at lunchtime and on most evenings June through August. Fuel up for the drive at **Lou Mitchell's** (www.loumitchellsrestaurant.com; 565 W Jackson Blvd; mains $6-11; 🕙5:30am-3pm Mon-Fri, 7am-3pm Sat & Sun; ♿; Ⓜ Blue Line to Clinton), slinging bacon and eggs since Route 66's heyday.

The Drive ›› Stay on Adams St for 1.5 miles until you come to Ogden Ave. Go left, and continue through the suburbs of Cicero and Berwyn. At Harlem Ave, turn left (south) and stay on it briefly

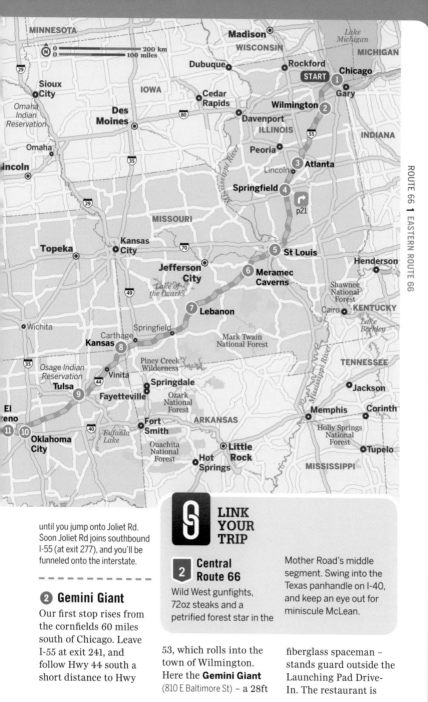

until you jump onto Joliet Rd. Soon Joliet Rd joins southbound I-55 (at exit 277), and you'll be funneled onto the interstate.

----

❷ Gemini Giant

Our first stop rises from the cornfields 60 miles south of Chicago. Leave I-55 at exit 241, and follow Hwy 44 south a short distance to Hwy

❽ LINK YOUR TRIP

2 Central Route 66

Wild West gunfights, 72oz steaks and a petrified forest star in the

53, which rolls into the town of Wilmington. Here the **Gemini Giant** (810 E Baltimore St) – a 28ft

Mother Road's middle segment. Swing into the Texas panhandle on I-40, and keep an eye out for miniscule McLean.

fiberglass spaceman – stands guard outside the Launching Pad Drive-In. The restaurant is now shuttered, but the humongous green rocket-holding statue remains a quintessential photo op.

The Drive » Head back to I-55 and take exit 154 for Funks Grove, a 19th-century maple-sirup farm (yes, that's sirup with an 'i'). Get on Old Route 66 (a frontage road that parallels the interstate here), and in 10 miles you'll reach Atlanta.

TRIP HIGHLIGHT

3 Atlanta

When you hear a collective 'mmm' rising from the cornfields, you'll know you've reached the throwback hamlet of Atlanta. Pull up a chair at the **Palms Grill Cafe** (☏217-648-2233; www.thepalmsgrillcafe.com; 110 SW Arch St; mains $5-8; ◷7am-7pm Tue-Sat), where thick slabs of gooseberry, chocolate cream and other retro pies tempt from the glass case. Then walk across the street to snap a photo with **Tall Paul**, a sky-high statue of Paul Bunyan clutching a hot dog. Stay on Arch St through town to see the old-fashioned murals that cover Atlanta's brick walls.

The Drive » Continue on Old Route 66 (the frontage road) for 10 miles to Lincoln and its sublime statue of Abraham Lincoln helming the world's largest covered wagon. You can try tracing the road for a while longer (it gets tricky), or return to I-55. Springfield is 30 miles onward.

4 Springfield (p59)

Illinois is the Land of Lincoln, according to local license plates, and the best place to get your Honest Abe fix is Springfield, the state capital. Fans of the 16th president get weak-kneed at the holy trio of sights: **Lincoln's Tomb** (www.lincolntomb.org; 1441 Monument Ave; ◷9am-5pm daily Apr-Aug, 9am-4:30pm Wed-Sat Sep-Mar), the **Lincoln Presidential Library & Museum** (☏217-558-8844; www.alplm.org; 212 N 6th St; adult/child $15/6; ◷9am-5pm; ♿) and the **Lincoln Home** (☏217-492-4150; www.nps.gov/liho; 426 S 7th St; ◷8:30am-5pm), all in or near downtown. And Springfield's Route 66 claim to fame? It's the birthplace of the corn dog (a cornmeal-battered, fried hot dog on a stick). The **Cozy Dog Drive In** (www.cozydogdrivein.com; 2935 S 6th St; mains $2-4.50; ◷8am-8pm Mon-Sat) is where the meaty goodness began, and the eatery is chock-full of route memorabilia.

The Drive » Return to I-55, which supersedes Route 66 here as in most of the state. Veer off for vintage cafes (in Litchfield) and restored gas stations (in Mt Olive). Near Edwardsville get on I-270, on which you'll swoop over the Mississippi River and enter Missouri.

5 St Louis (p60)

Just over the border is St Louis, a can-do city that has launched westbound travelers for centuries. To ogle the city's most iconic attraction, exit I-270 onto Riverview Dr and point your car south toward the 630ft-tall **Gateway Arch** (www.gatewayarch.com; tram ride adult/child $10/5; ◷8am-10pm Jun-Aug, 9am-6pm Sep-May), a graceful reminder of the city's role in westward expansion. For up-close views of the stainless-steel span and the Jefferson National Expansion Memorial surrounding it, turn left onto Washington Ave from Tucker Blvd (12th St). West of the center, **Ted Drewes** (www.teddrewes.com; 6726 Chippewa St; cones 60c to $2.80; ◷11am-11pm Feb-Dec) has been serving frozen custard to generations of Route 66 roadies. Get in line at the icicle-trimmed shack to order a 'concrete' – an ice-creamy concoction so thick they hand it to you upside down.

The Drive » From here, I-44 closely tracks – and often covers – chunks of original Mother Road. Take the interstate southwest to Stanton, then follow the signs to Meramec Caverns.

6 Meramec Caverns

Admit it: you're curious. Kitschy billboards have been touting **Meramec**

Caverns (www.americascave.com; Exit 230 off I-44; adult/child $21/11; ⏱8:30am-7:30pm summer, reduced hours rest of year) for miles. The family-mobbed attraction and campground has lured road-trippers with its offbeat ads since 1933. From gold panning to riverboat rides, you'll find a day's worth of distractions, but don't miss the historically and geologically engaging cave tour. Note to kitsch-seekers: the restaurant and gift store are actually inside the mouth of the cave.

The Drive » Route 66 follows a series of winding county roads through wee towns such as Bourbon, Cuba and Devil's Elbow, all sticking close to I-44. After 100 miles or so, Lebanon makes a swell pit stop.

- - - - - - - - - - - - -

TRIP HIGHLIGHT

❼ Lebanon

Most folks pull into town for the **Munger Moss Motel** (☎417-532-3111; www.mungermoss.com; 1336 E Rte 66; r from $50; ❈🛜🐾). The 1940s lodging has a monster of a neon sign and atmospheric rooms, but more importantly it has Mother Road–loving owners who've been welcoming travelers for over 40 years. They can point you to the town's best root beer and antique shops, the top spots to canoe amid the gorgeous Ozark hills, and the prime times to bowl at the alley

across the street. The **Route 66 Museum & Research Center** (www.lebanon-laclede.lib.mo.us; 915 S Jefferson St; ⏱8am-8pm Mon-Thu, to 5pm Fri & Sat) at Lebanon's library has a cool collection, including a vintage car and gas pump.

The Drive » Ditch I-44 west of Springfield, taking Hwy 96 to Civil War–era Carthage with its historic town square and 66 Drive-In Theatre. From Joplin, follow Hwy 66 to Old Route 66 then hold tight: Kansas is on the horizon.

- - - - - - - - - - - - -

❽ Kansas (p65)

The tornado-prone state holds a mere 13 miles of Mother Road (less than 1% of the total) but there's still a lot to see. First you'll pass through mine-scarred **Galena**, where a rusty old tow truck inspired animators from Pixar to create the character Mater in *Cars*. A few miles later, stop at the red-brick **Eisler**

Brothers Old Riverton Store (☎620-848-3330; www.eislerbros.com; 7109 SE Hwy 66; ⏱7:30am-8pm Mon-Sat, noon-7pm Sun) and stock up on batteries, turkey sandwiches and Route 66 memorabilia. The 1925 property looks much like it did when built – note the pressed-tin ceiling and the outhouse – and it's on the National Register of Historic Places. Cross Hwy 400 and continue to the **1923 Marsh Rainbow Arch Bridge**, from where it's 3 miles south to **Baxter Springs**, site of a Civil War massacre and numerous bank robberies.

The Drive » Enter Oklahoma. From Afton, Route 66 parallels I-44 (now a tollway) through Vinita, home to Clanton's famed chicken-fried-steak cafe. Another 40 miles brings you to Claremore, home of cowboy Will Rogers, then to Catoosa, where the 80ft-long Blue Whale attracts camera-happy crowds. Tulsa rolls up soon after.

↱ DETOUR:
OLD CHAIN OF ROCKS BRIDGE

Start: ❹ **Springfield**

Before driving into Missouri, detour off I-270 at exit 3. Follow Hwy 3 (aka Lewis and Clark Blvd) south, turn right at the first stoplight and drive west to the 1929 **Old Chain of Rocks Bridge** (Old Chain of Rocks Rd; ⏱9am-dusk). Open only to pedestrians and cyclists these days, the mile-long span over the Mississippi River has a 22-degree angled bend (the cause of many a crash, hence the ban on cars). Hide your valuables and lock your car if you leave it to go exploring.

LOCAL KNOWLEDGE:
KNOW YOUR PIE
KARLA ZIMMERMAN, AUTHOR

Route 66 is not only the Mother Road, but the mother lode when it comes to pie. Sweet-tart green gooseberries are often baked between crusts, like in Atlanta's Palms Grill Cafe. Pecan pie is Oklahoma's official favorite; it's part of the 'state meal.' Cream pies are the region's masterwork: banana cream, coconut cream and chocolate cream tempt at many diners.

Above: 1969 Oldsmobile convertible
Above right: pecan pie

❾ Tulsa (p65)
East 11th St takes you into and right through art-deco-rich Tulsa; be sure to look for the iconic neon wonder of the restored **Meadow Gold sign** at S Quaker Ave. To get a feel for what the city was like in its Route 66 days, head to the **Brady Arts District**, across the train

tracks from downtown. Music clubs from the era still swing, and offbeat museums devoted to **Woody Guthrie** (www. woodyguthriecenter.org; 102 E Brady St; adult/child $8/6; ⏰10am-6pm Tue-Sun) and local jazz players impress.

The Drive » The rural route from Tulsa to Oklahoma City is one of the longest continuous stretches of Mother Road

remaining (110 miles), a fine alternative to the I-44 tollway. As it approaches Oklahoma City, Route 66 follows Hwy 77 into town.

----

⑩ Oklahoma City (p67)

Bobby Troup called the city 'mighty pretty' in his classic tune 'Route 66,' but OKC is more cowboy than comely. Get

in the spirit at **National Cowboy & Western Heritage Museum** (www. nationalcowboymuseum.org; 1700 NE 63rd St; adult/child $12.50/6; ⏰10am-5pm). Other boots-and-chaps attractions are corralled south of downtown in Stockyards City, where you can watch a cattle auction, buy a custom-made cowboy hat or carve into savory

23

TOP TIP:
ROAD RESOURCES BY STATE

For those on the lookout for even more quirky stops, antique bridges or folk-art marvels, these groups provide additional information for road-tripping in the region:

Route 66 Association of Illinois (www.il66assoc.org)

Route 66 Association of Missouri (www.missouri66.org)

Oklahoma Route 66 Association (www.oklahomaroute66.com)

Route 66 Association of Texas (www.route66oftexas.com)

sirloin. The Field of Empty Chairs at the **Oklahoma City National Memorial Museum** (www.oklahomacitynationalmemorial.org; 620 N Harvey Ave; adult/student $12/10; 9am-6pm Mon-Sat, noon-6pm Sun) is a moving reminder of those killed by a terrorist explosion here on April 19, 1995. On your way out of town, mosey into **Ann's Chicken Fry House** (4106 NW 39th St; mains $4-12; 11am-8:30pm Tue-Sat) for the time-honored specialty with cream gravy.

The Drive » From OKC, Route 66 follows Business I-40 for 20 miles to El Reno and its distinctive meat. Sniff your way into town...

11 El Reno

The first fried-onion burger was served in 1926 in El Reno. Today, the kick'n delicacy (ground beef combined with raw onions then caramelized on the grill) is a town staple. Among several historic drive-ins and dives, try **Johnnie's Grill** (301 S Rock Island; 9am-7pm) or **Sid's** (300 S Choctaw Ave; 11am-7pm). Sid's has outdoor tables, Johnnie's has the bigger dining area.

The Drive » The route hugs I-40, sometimes paralleling it to the the north, through 60 miles of lonesome landscapes to Clinton.

TRIP HIGHLIGHT

12 Oklahoma Route 66 Museum

Flags from all eight Mother Road states fly high beside the memorabilia-filled **Oklahoma Route 66 Museum** (580-323-7866; www.route66.org; 2229 W Gary Blvd; adult/child $5/1; 9am-7pm Mon-Sat, 1-6pm Sun summer, reduced hours rest of year;) in Clinton. This fun-loving treasure trove, run by the Oklahoma Historical Society, isn't your typical mishmash of photos, clippings and knickknacks (though there is an artifact-filled Cabinet of Curios). Instead, it uses music and videos to dramatize six decades of Route 66 history.

Central Route 66

2

Concrete wigwams. A neon cowboy. Lumbering dinosaurs. 'Get Your Kitsch on Route 66' might be the best slogan for the scrubby patch of Mother Road connecting Texas, New Mexico and Arizona.

TRIP HIGHLIGHTS

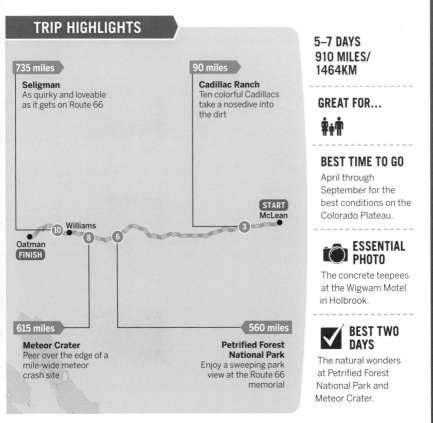

735 miles
Seligman
As quirky and loveable as it gets on Route 66

90 miles
Cadillac Ranch
Ten colorful Cadillacs take a nosedive into the dirt

Williams
Oatman
FINISH
START
McLean

615 miles
Meteor Crater
Peer over the edge of a mile-wide meteor crash site

560 miles
Petrified Forest National Park
Enjoy a sweeping park view at the Route 66 memorial

5–7 DAYS
910 MILES/ 1464KM

GREAT FOR...

BEST TIME TO GO
April through September for the best conditions on the Colorado Plateau.

ESSENTIAL PHOTO
The concrete teepees at the Wigwam Motel in Holbrook.

BEST TWO DAYS
The natural wonders at Petrified Forest National Park and Meteor Crater.

Left Seligman, Arizona

2 Central Route 66

The Snow Cap Drive-In encapsulates everything that's cool about Route 66. There's personal interaction — did the guy behind the counter just squirt me with fake mustard? It's old-fashioned — why yes, I will get a malt. And it draws a diverse sampling of humanity — from a busload of bleary-eyed tourists to a horde of tough-looking biker dudes, all linked at the Snow Cap by the simple joy of an ice-cream cone.

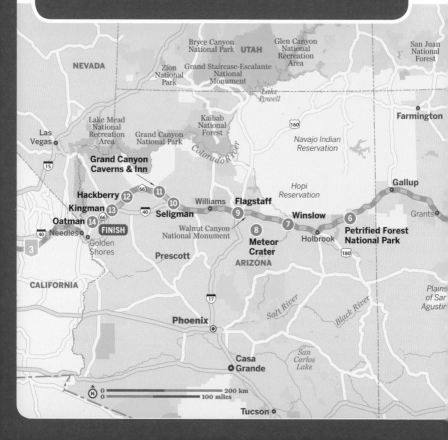

1 McLean

Beyond the towns, the great wide open of the Texas Panhandle is punctuated only by the occasional windmill, and the distinct odor of cattle feedlots in the distance. The Mother Road cuts across this emptiness for 178 miles, and the entire route has been replaced by I-40 – but there are a few noteworthy attractions.

The sprawling grasslands of Texas and other western cattle states were once open range, where steers and cowboys could wander where they darn well pleased. That all changed in the 1880s when the devil's rope – more commonly known as barbed wire – began dividing up the land into private parcels. The **Devil's Rope Museum** (www.barbwiremuseum.com; 100 Kingsley St; admission free; ⏰9am-5pm Mon-Fri, 10am-4pm Sat Mar-Nov) in the battered town of McLean off exit 141 has vast barbed wire displays and a small but homey and idiosyncratic room devoted to Route 66. The detailed map of the road in Texas is a must. Also worth a look are the moving portraits of Dust Bowl damage and refugees from human-made environmental disaster.

The Drive ›› I-40 west of McLean glides over low-rolling hills. The landscape flattens at Groom, home of the tilting water tower and a 19-story cross at exit 112. Take exit 96 for Conway to snap a photo of the forlorn VW Beetle Ranch, aka the Bug Ranch, on the south side of the interstate. Take exit 74.

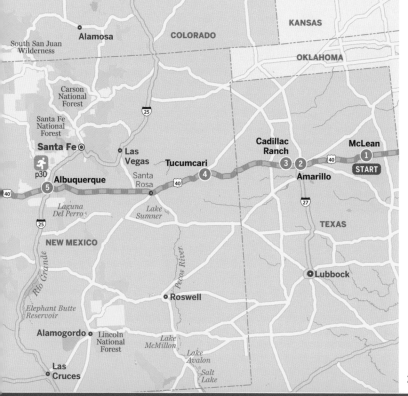

2 Amarillo

This cowboy town holds a plethora of Route 66 sites: the **Big Texan Steak Ranch** (www.bigtexan.com; 7701 I-40 E, exit 74; mains $10-40; ⊘7am-10.30pm; ⊞), the historic livestock auction and the San Jacinto District, which still has original Route 66 businesses.

As for the Big Texan, this hokey but classic attraction opened on Route 66 in 1960. It moved to its current location after I-40 opened in 1971 and has never looked back. The attention-grabbing gimmick here is the 'free 72oz steak' offer – you have to eat this enormous portion of cow plus a multitude of sides in under one hour, or you pay for the entire meal ($72). Contestants sit at a raised table to 'entertain' the other diners. Less than 20% pass the challenge. Insane eating

aside, the ranch is a fine place to eat, and the steaks are excellent.

The Drive » Continue west on I-40. Take exit 60, about 5 miles west of the edge of downtown Amarillo, then backtrack a mile on the southern frontage road from the Love's gas station.

TRIP HIGHLIGHT

3 Cadillac Ranch

Controversial local millionaire Stanley Marsh planted the shells of 10 Cadillacs in the deserted ground west of Amarillo in 1974 – an installation that's come to be known as Cadillac Ranch. He said he created it as a tribute to the golden age of car travel. The cars date from 1948 to 1959 – a period in which tail fins just kept getting bigger and bigger. Come prepared: the accepted practice is to leave your own mark by spray painting on the

cars. It can also get quite windy.

The Drive » Follow I-40 west 60 miles to the New Mexico border. Tucumcari – and its 1200+ motel rooms – is 40 miles west.

4 Tucumcari (p71)

A ranching and farming town sandwiched between the mesas and the plains, Tucumcari is home to one of the best-preserved sections of Route 66 in the country. It's a great place to drive through at night, when dozens of neon signs – relics of the town's Route 66 heyday – cast a crazy rainbow-colored glow. Tucumcari's Route 66 motoring legacy and other regional highlights are recorded on 35 murals in downtown and the surrounding area. Pick up a map for the murals at the **Chamber of Commerce** (☎575-461-1694; www.tucumcarinm.com; 404 W Route 66; ⊘8:30am-5pm Mon-Fri).

The engaging **Mesalands Dinosaur Museum** (www.mesalands.edu/community/dinosaur-museum; 222 E Laughlin St; adult/child $6.50/4; ⊘10am-6pm Tue-Sat Mar-Aug, noon-5pm Tue-Sat Sep-Feb; ⊞) showcases real dinosaur bones and has hands-on exhibits for kids. Casts of dinosaur bones are done in bronze (not the usual plaster of paris), which shows fine detail.

↱ DETOUR: SANTA FE

Start: 5 Albuquerque

New Mexico's capital city is an oasis of art and culture lifted 7000ft above sea level, against the backdrop of the Sangre de Christo Mountains. It was on Route 66 until 1938, when a realignment left it by the wayside. It's well worth the detour to see the Georgia O'Keeffe Museum and to fork into uber-hot green chili dishes in the superb restaurants. See p85 for more. Route 66 follows the Old Pecos Trail (NM466) into town.

The Drive » West on I-40, dry and windy plains spread into the distance, the horizon interrupted by flat-topped mesas. To stretch your legs, take exit 273 from Route 66/I-40 to downtown Santa Rosa and the Route 66 Auto Museum, which has upwards of 35 cars from the 1920s through the 1960s, all in beautiful condition.

- - - - - - - - - - - -

⑤ Albuquerque (p73)

After 1936, Route 66 was re-aligned from its original path, which linked north through Santa Fe, to a direct line west into Albuquerque. Today, the city's Central Ave follows the post-1937 route. It passes through Nob Hill, the university, downtown and Old Town.

The patioed **Kelly's Brewery** (www.kellysbrewpub.com; 3222 Central Ave SE; ⊙8am-10:30pm Sun-Thu, 8am-midnight Fri & Sat), in trendy Nob Hill, was an Art Moderne gas station on the route, commissioned in 1939. West of I-25, look for the spectacular tile-and-wood artistry of the **KiMo Theatre** (☏505-768-3544; www.cabq.gov/kimo; 423 Central Ave NW, Downtown), across from the old Indian trading post. This 1927 icon of pueblo deco architecture blends Native American culture with art-deco design. It also screens classic movies like *Singin' in the*

GALLUP MURAL WALK

Take a walk around Gallup – begin at City Hall on the corner of W Aztec Ave and S 2nd St – and experience her 131-year-old story through art. Many buildings around this old Route 66 town double as canvases, sporting giant murals, both abstract and realist, that memorialize special events in Gallup's roller-coaster history. The city's mural painting tradition started in the 1930s as part of President Franklin D Roosevelt's Great Depression Work Projects Administration (WPA) program.

Rain and *2001: A Space Odyssey*. For prehistoric designs, take exit 154, just west of downtown, and drive north 3 miles to **Petroglyph National Monument** (☏505-899-0205; www.nps.gov/petr; 6001 Unser Blvd NW; ⊙ visitor center 8am-5pm), which has more than 20,000 rock etchings.

The Drive » Route 66 dips from I-40 into Gallup, becoming the main drag past beautifully renovated buildings, including the 1926 Spanish Colonial El Morro Theater. From Gallup, it's 21 miles to Arizona. In Arizona, take exit 311 to enter Petrified Forest National Park.

- - - - - - - - - - - -

TRIP HIGHLIGHT

⑥ Petrified Forest National Park (p90)

The 'trees' of the **Petrified Forest** (☏928-524-6228; www.nps.gov/pefo; vehicle/walk-in, bicycle & motorcycle $10/5; ⊙7am-8pm Jun & Jul, shorter hours Aug-May) are fragmented, fossilized 225-million-year-old logs scattered over a vast area of semidesert grassland.

Many are huge – up to 6ft in diameter – and at least one spans a ravine to form a natural bridge. The trees arrived via major floods, only to be buried beneath silica-rich volcanic ash before they could decompose. Groundwater dissolved the silica, carried it through the logs and crystallized into solid, sparkly quartz mashed up with iron, carbon, manganese and other minerals. Uplift and erosion eventually exposed the logs.

The park, which straddles the I-40, has an entrance at exit 311 in the north and another off Hwy 180 in the south. A 28-mile paved scenic road, Park Rd, links the two. To avoid backtracking, westbound travelers should start in the north, eastbound travelers in the south.

The Drive » Drive west 25 miles to Holbrook, a former Wild West town now home to rock shops and the photo-ready Wigwam Motel, which was

LOCAL KNOWLEDGE: KINGMAN TO SELIGMAN
AMY C BALFOUR, AUTHOR

My favorite section of Route 66 is the 115-mile stretch from Kingman east to Seligman. Things get quirky fast. You suddenly want to race a train. Tiny Hackberry draws an international crowd. Up pops a town called Valentine followed by a fake dinosaur. All linked by nutty Burma Shave signs. Then, for the finale, you get trapped inside Snow Cap Drive-In because you can't open the trick door.

Top: Vintage Route 66 sign, Kingman
Left: General store, Hackberry, Arizona
Right: Roadside mailboxes, Kingman

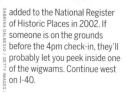

added to the National Register of Historic Places in 2002. If someone is on the grounds before the 4pm check-in, they'll probably let you peek inside one of the wigwams. Continue west on I-40.

- - - - - - - - - -

⑦ Winslow (p91)

'Standing on a corner in Winslow, Arizona...' Sound familiar? Thanks to The Eagles' 1972 tune 'Take It Easy' (written by Jackson Browne and Glenn Frey), lonesome little Winslow is now a popular stop on the tourist track. Pose with the life-sized bronze statue of a hitchhiker backed by a charmingly hokey trompe l'oeil mural of that famous 'girl – my Lord! – in a flatbed Ford' at the corner of 2nd St and Kinsley Ave.

The Drive » Twenty miles west of Winslow, take exit 233 off I-40 and drive 6 miles south.

- - - - - - - - - -

⑧ Meteor Crater

A fiery meteor crashed here 50,000 years ago, blasting a hole some 550ft deep and nearly 1 mile across. Today the privately owned **crater** (☎928-289-5898; www.meteorcrater.com; adult/senior/6-17yr $18/16/9; ⊙7am-7pm Jun–mid-Sep, 8am-5pm mid-Sep–May) is a major tourist attraction with exhibits about meteorites, crater geology and the Apollo astronauts who used its lunar-like surface to train for their moon missions. You're not allowed to go down into the crater, but there are a few look-out points as well as guided one-hour rim walking tours (free with admission). Look for the glinting piece of a plane that crashed inside the crater.

The Drive » Follow I-40 to exit 204 and pick up Route 66 into Flagstaff. This is also the exit for Walnut Canyon National Monument (p92). From the east, Route 66 passes a lengthy swath of cheap indie motels as well as the boot-kickin' Museum Club (3404 E Rte 66), a log-cabin-style roadhouse that's been entertaining roadtrippers since 1936. Chug into downtown Flagstaff alongside the railroad tracks.

9 Flagstaff (p92)

This cultured college town still has an Old West heart. At the visitor center, which is inside the old train depot, pick up the free Route 66 walking tour guide. One of the buildings on the tour is the **Downtowner Motel**, formerly a brothel and now the Grand Canyon International Youth Hostel. Just north of Route 66 are two century-old hotels: the **Hotel Monte Vista** and the **Weatherford**. Both have plenty of character, not to mention convivial watering holes and lively ghosts.

If you're interested in architecture, stop by **Riordan Mansion State Historic Park** (☎928-779-

4395; www.azstateparks.com/parks/rima; 409 W Riordan Rd; adult/child 7-13yr $10/5; ⏰9:30am-5pm May-Oct, 10:30am-5pm Thu-Mon Nov-Apr) just south. Having made a fortune from their Arizona Lumber Company, brothers Micahel and Timothy Riordan had this house built in 1904. The mansion's Craftsman-style design was the brainchild of architect Charles Whittlesey, who designed El Tovar on the South Rim.

The Drive » Route 66 rejoins I-40 just west of Flagstaff. Continue 30 miles to Williams, home of the Grand Canyon Railway and the Red Garter Bed & Bakery. Williams was the last community along Route 66 to be bypassed by I-40. Route 66 runs one way in Williams, from west to east. Railroad Ave parallels Route 66 and heads one way west. Rejoin I-40, only to leave it again at exit 139.

TRIP HIGHLIGHT

10 Seligman (p97)

This town takes its Route 66 heritage seriously – or with a squirt of fake mustard – thanks to the Delgadillo brothers, who for decades were the Mother Road's biggest boosters. Juan sadly passed away in 2004, but nonagenarian Angel and his wife Vilma still run **Angel's Barbershop** (☎928-422-3352; www.route66giftshop.com; 217 E Rte 66; ⏰9am-5pm), where

SCENIC DRIVE: PETRIFIED FOREST NATIONAL PARK

The leisurely Park Rd, which travels through the park, has about 15 pullouts with interpretive signs and some short trails. North of I-40, enjoy sweeping views of the Painted Desert, where nature presents a hauntingly beautiful palette, especially at sunset. After Park Rd turns south, keep a lookout for the roadside display about Route 66, just north of the interstate.

The 3-mile loop drive out to Blue Mesa has 360-degree views of spectacular badlands, log falls and logs balancing atop hills with the leathery texture of elephant skin.

Two trails near the southern entrance provide the best access for close-ups of the petrified logs: the 0.6-mile Long Logs Trail, which has the largest concentration, and the 0.4-mile Giant Logs Trail, which is entered through the Rainbow Forest Museum and sports the park's largest log.

you can poke around for souvenirs and admire license plates sent in by fans from all over the world. Angel's madcap brother Juan used to rule supreme over the **Snow Cap Drive-In** (☏928-422-3291; 301 E Rte 66; dishes $3.25-6.25; ⏱10am-6pm mid-Mar–Nov), a Route 66 institution serving burgers, ice cream and pranks, now run by his sons Bob and John.

The Drive » The Mother Road rolls northwest through scrub-covered desert, passing Burma Shave signs and lonely trains. Kitsch roars its dinosaury head at mile marker 115.

- - - - - - - - - - -

⓫ Grand Canyon Caverns & Inn (p97)

An elevator drops 210ft underground to artificially lit limestone caverns and the skeletal remains of a prehistoric ground sloth at **Grand Canyon Caverns** (☏928-422-3223; www.gccaverns. com; Rte 66, mile marker 115; 45 min tour adult/child $20/13; ⏱9am-5pm Jun-Sep, 10am-5pm Oct-May; 👪). If you've seen other caverns, these might not be as impressive, but kids get a kick out of a visit. A shorter, wheelchair-accessible tour is also available (adult/child $16/11). Since 2010, the property has offered its Cavern Suite ($800) as an overnight lodging option. This underground 'room' has

HISTORY OF ROUTE 66

Launched in 1926, Route 66 stretched from Chicago to Los Angeles, linking a ribbon of small towns and country byways as it rolled across eight states. The road gained notoriety during the Great Depression when migrant farmers followed it west from the Dust Bowl across the Great Plains. The nickname 'The Mother Road' first appeared in John Steinbeck's novel about the era, *The Grapes of Wrath*. Meanwhile unemployed young men were hired to pave the final stretches of muddy road. They completed the job, as it turns out, just in time for WWII. Hitchhiking soldiers and factory workers rode the road next. Things got a little more fun after WWII when newfound prosperity prompted Americans to hit the open road. Sadly, just as things got going, the Feds rolled out the interstate system, which eventually caused the Mother Road's demise. The very last town to be bypassed by an interstate was Arizona's very own Williams, in 1984.

two double beds, a sitting area and multicolored lamps. If you ever wanted to live in one of those postapocalyptic sci-fi movies, here's your chance! One of the DVDs on offer is an underground horror flick – watch it here only if you're especially twisted.

The Drive » Continue west through Peach Springs, Truxton and Valentine, for 35 miles.

- - - - - - - - - - - -

⓬ Hackberry (p97)

Teensy Hackberry is one of the few still-kicking settlements on this segment of the Mother Road's original alignment. Inside an eccentrically remodeled gas station is the **Hackberry General Store** (☏928-769-2605; www. hackberrygeneralstore.com; 11255 E Rte 66; admission free;

⏱typically 8am-6pm). The life's work of highway memorialist Robert Waldmire, the building started as a general store in 1934, and is a great place to stop for an ice-cold Coke and Mother Road memorabilia. Check out the vintage petrol pumps, cars faded by decades of hot desert light, old toilet seats and rusted-out ironwork.

The Drive » From here, Route 66 arcs southwest, back toward I-40, then barrels into Kingman, which is 27 miles away.

- - - - - - - - - - -

⓭ Kingman (p97)

Founded in the heady 1880s railway days, Kingman is a quiet place today. The visitor center is at the western end of Kingman, in a 1907 powerhouse. The

ROUTE 66 READS

John Steinbeck's *Grapes of Wrath* is the classic novel of travel on the Mother Road during the Dust Bowl era. Woody Guthrie's *Bound for Glory* is the road-trip autobiography of a folk singer during the Depression. Several museums and bookshops along Route 66 stock Native American, Old West and pioneer writing with ties to the old highway.

building also holds the small but engaging **Route 66 Museum** (☏928-753-9889; www.kingmantourism.org; 120 W Andy Devine Ave; adult/senior/child 12yr & under $4/3/ free; ⏰9am-5pm), which has a great historical overview of the Mother Road. Check out the **former Methodist church** at 5th and Spring St where Clark Gable and Carole Lombard tied the knot.

In Kingman Route 66 is also called Andy Devine Ave, named after the hometown hero who acted in Hollywood classics like *Stagecoach*, in which he played the perpetually befuddled stagecoach driver.

The Drive » Route 66 corkscrews up a claustrophobic canyon and the rugged Black Mountains then passes falling rocks, cacti and tumbleweeds on its way over Sitgreaves Pass (3523ft) and into the old mining town of Oatman.

⓮ Oatman (p99)

Since the veins of ore ran dry in 1942, crusty Oatman has reinvented itself as a movie set and Wild West tourist trap, complete with staged gun fights (daily at 1:30pm and 3:30pm) and gift stores named Fast Fanny's Place and the Classy Ass.

Speaking of asses, there are plenty of them (the four-legged kind, that is) roaming the streets. Stupid and endearing, they're the descendants of pack animals left by the early miners. These burros may beg for food, but do not feed them carrots. Instead, buy healthier hay cubes for $1 per bag at nearby stores. Squeezed among the shops is the 1902 **Oatman Hotel**, a surprisingly modest shack (no longer renting rooms) where Clark Gable and Carole Lombard spent their wedding night in 1939. On July 4 the town holds a sidewalk egg-frying contest. Now that's hot!

From here, Route 66 twists down to Golden Shores and I-40.

Right Antique shop, Oatman, Arizona

STEPHEN SAKS / GETTY IMAGES ©

Western Route 66

3

From historic Needles in the east through to the sparkling waters of the mighty Pacific, search for your own American dream along California's stretch of the Mother Road.

TRIP HIGHLIGHTS

300 miles

Hollywood
Get your kicks in Tinseltown

80 miles

Amboy
The big sky and empty byways are starkly photogenic

START
Needles

3

● Victorville

San
● Bernardino

10
11 ● Los Angeles
FINISH

Santa Monica
End this epic trip on the Pacific shore

310 miles

3–4 DAYS
223 MILES/375KM

GREAT FOR...

BEST TIME TO GO
Spring, when you can cruise with the windows down before the heat of summer.

ESSENTIAL PHOTO
Lying down on the faded blacktop next to the Route 66 signs.

BEST ROAD
National Trails Hwy between Goffs and Amboy is the quintessential middle-of-nowhere cruise.

Left Abandoned gas station, Route 66

3 Western Route 66

For generations of Americans, California, with its sparkling waters and sunny skies, was the promised land for road-trippers on Route 66. Follow their tracks through the gauntlet of Mojave Desert ghost towns, railway whistle-stops like Barstow and Victorville, and across the Cajon Summit. Finally, wind down the LA Basin, and put it in park near the crashing ocean waves at the end of Santa Monica Pier.

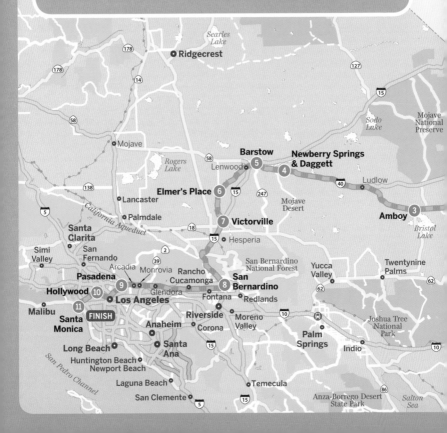

1 Needles

At the Arizona border south of I-40 the **Old Trails Arch Bridge** (off I-40 exit 1, east of the California-Arizona border; ⊘ no public access) welcomes the Mother Road to California under endless blue skies. You might recognize the bridge: the Depression-era Joad family used it to cross the Colorado River in the movie version of John Steinbeck's novel *Grapes of Wrath*. Drive west past **Needles**, a

dusty throwback railroad town with a historic depot down by the river. Frozen in a half-restored state, the **El Graces Depot** is one of only a few frontier-era Harvey Houses left standing in the American West. The Harvey Houses were a chain of railway hotels and restaurant popular in the late 19th and early 20th centuries that were famed for traveling waitresses – portrayed by Judy Garland in the 1949 MGM musical *The Harvey Girls*. Head a bit south on Broadway and you'll pass a freshly restored **66 Motel Sign** at the corner of Desnok St – a great photo.

The Drive >> West of Needles, follow Hwy 95 north of I-40 for 6 miles, then turn left onto Goffs Rd. You'll inevitably be running alongside a long locomotive – this is a primary rail shipping route to the West Coast.

2 Goffs

The shade of cottonwood trees make the 1914 Mission-style **Goffs Schoolhouse** (☏760-733-4482; www.mdhca.org; 37198 Lanfair Rd; donations welcome; ⊘ usually 9am-4pm Sat & Sun) a soothing stop along this sun-drenched stretch of highway. It stands as part of the best-preserved pioneer settlement in the Mojave Desert (although to be quite honest it looks a bit like an empty Taco Bell). Browsing the black-

and-white photographs of hardscrabble Dust Bowl migrants gives an evocative glimpse into tough life on the edge of the Mojave.

The Drive >> Keep going on Goffs Rd through Fenner, crossing under I-40. Turn right onto National Old Trails Hwy (which is also known as National Trails Hwy on some maps and signs) and drive for about an hour. This is some of the coolest stretch of road, with abandoned graffiti-covered service stations, vintage signs rusting in the sun and huge skies.

TRIP HIGHLIGHT

3 Amboy

Potholed and crumbling in a romantic way, the USA's original transnational highway was established in 1912, more than a decade before Route 66 first ran through here. The rutted highway races through tiny towns, sparsely scattered across the Mojave. Only a few landmarks interrupt the horizon, including **Roy's Motel & Cafe** (www.rt66roys. com; National Old Trails Hwy; admission free; ⊘ vary), a landmark watering hole for decades of Route 66 travelers. If you'll believe the lore, Roy once cooked his famous Route 66 double cheeseburger on the hood of a '63 Mercury. Although the motel is abandoned, the gas station and cafe are occasionally open. It's east of **Amboy Crater**

(☎760-326-7000; www.blm.gov/ca; 1 mile west of Amboy; admission free; ☉sunrise-sunset), an almost perfectly symmetrical volcanic cinder cone. You can hike to the top, but it's best to avoid the midday sun – the 1.5-mile hike doesn't have a stitch of shade.

The Drive » From Amboy travel along National Old Trails Highway to Ludlow, a trip of 30 miles. At Ludlow, turn right onto Crucero Rd and pass under I-40, then take the north frontage road west and turn left at Lavic Rd. Back on the south side of I-40, keep heading west on the National Old Trails Hwy. This entire trip will take about one hour and 45 minutes.

❹ Newberry Springs & Daggett

The highway passes under I-40 again on its way through **Daggett**, site of the harsh California inspection station faced by Dust Bowl refugees in *Grapes of Wrath*. Today, there ain't much action, but it's a windswept, picturesque place. Pay your respects to early desert adventurers at the old **Stone Hotel** (National Old Trails Hwy, Daggett; ☉no public entry). This late-19th-century hotel once housed miners, desert explorers and wanderers, including Sierra Nevada naturalist John Muir and Death Valley Scotty. Then make your way out of town to visit the **Calico Ghost Town** (☎800-862-2542; www.calicotown.com; 36600 Ghost Town Rd, Yermo; adult/child $8/5; ☉9am-5pm; 👪). This endearingly hokey Old West attraction sets a cluster of reconstructed pioneer-era buildings amid ruins of a late-19th-century silver mining town. You'll pay extra to go gold panning, tour the Maggie Mine or ride a narrow-gauge railway. Old-timey heritage celebrations include Civil War re-enactments and a bluegrass 'hootenanny.'

The Drive » Drive west to Nebo Rd, turning left to rejoin I-40. You'll drive about 15 minutes before taking the exit for Barstow Road.

❺ Barstow (p108)

Exit the interstate onto Main St, which runs through Barstow, a railroad settlement and historic crossroads, where murals adorn empty buildings downtown. Follow 1st St north across the Mojave River over a trestle bridge to the 1911 Harvey House, nicknamed 'Casa del Desierto,' designed by Western architect Mary Colter. Next to a small railroad museum is the **Route 66 'Mother Road' Museum** (☎760-255-1890; www.route66museum.org; 681 N 1st St, Barstow; donations welcome; ☉10am-4pm Fri & Sat, 11am-4pm Sun, or by appointment), displaying black-and-white historical photographs and odds and ends of everyday life in the early 20th century. Back in the day, it was also a Harvey House.

The Drive » Leaving Barstow via Main St, rejoin the National Old Trails Hwy west. It curves alongside the Mojave River through Lenwood. After 25 minutes you'll arrive at Elmer's Place.

❻ Elmer's Place

Loved by Harley bikers, this rural byway is like a scavenger hunt for Mother Road ruins, including antique filling stations and tumbledown

TOP TIP: NAVIGATING THE MOTHER ROAD

As you might imagine, nostalgia for the Mother Road draws its shares of completists who want to drive every inch. For Route 66 enthusiasts who need to cover every mile, a free turn-by-turn driving guide is available online at www.historic66.com. Also surf to www.route66ca.org for more historical background, photos and info about special events.

motor courts. Colorful as a box of crayons, **Elmer's Place** (24266 National Trails Hwy; ⏰24hr) is a roadside folk-art collection of 'bottle trees,' made from recycled soda pop and beer containers, telephone poles and railroad signs. Elmer Long, who was a career man at the cement factory you'll pass just out of town, is the proprietor and cracked artistic genius. If you see someone with a long white beard and leathery skin cementing a statue of a bronze deity to some elk antlers, you've found the right guy. Want to leave a little part of yourself along Route 66? Bring a little something for Elmer Long's colorful forest, constructed lovingly out of little pieces of junk.

The Drive » Cross over the Mojave River on a 1930s steel-truss bridge, then roll into downtown Victorville, a trip of about 20 minutes.

- - - - - - - - - - - -

⑦ Victorville

Opposite the railroad tracks in quiet little Victorville, visitors poke around a mishmash of historical exhibits and contemporary art inside the **California Route 66 Museum** (☏760-951-0436; www.califrt66museum.org; 16825 D St; donations welcome; ⏰10am-4pm Thu-Sat & Mon, 11am-3pm Sun). The museum building itself was once the Red Rooster

Cafe, a famous Route 66 roadhouse. It's a bit of a cluttered nostalgia trip – piled with old signs and roadside memorabilia – but worth a quick look.

The Drive » Get back on I-15 south over the daunting Cajon Summit. Descending into San Bernardino, take I-215 and exit at Devore. Follow Cajon Blvd to Mt Vernon Ave, detour east on Base Line St and go left onto 'E' St. This trip takes about 40 minutes. If you're hungry, pull off in Hesperia at the Summit Inn, a classic diner.

- - - - - - - - - - - -

⑧ San Bernardino

Look for the Golden Arches outside the **First McDonald's Museum** (☏909-885-6324; 1398 N E St; ⏰10am-5pm). It was here that salesman Ray Kroc dropped in to sell Dick and Mac McDonald a mixer. Eventually Kroc bought the rights to the brothers' name and built an empire. Half of the museum is devoted to Route 66, with particularly interesting photographs and maps. Turn west on 5th St, leaving San Bernardino via Foothill Blvd, which continues straight into the urban sprawl of greater Los Angeles. It's a long haul west to Pasadena, with stop-and-go traffic most of the way, but there are more than a handful of gems to uncover. Cruising through Fontana, birthplace of the Hells Angels biker club, pause for a photo by the **Giant Orange** (15395 Foothill

Blvd, Fontana; ⏰no public entry), a 1920s juice stand of the kind that was once a fixture alongside SoCal's citrus groves.

The Drive » Stay on Route 66 as it detours briefly onto Alosta Ave. Take lunch in Glendora, and shortly after 66 rejoins Foothill Blvd in Azusa. Continue onto Huntington Dr in Duarte, where a boisterous Route 66 parade happens in mid-September.

- - - - - - - - - - - -

⑨ Pasadena (p107)

Just before you reach Pasadena, you'll pass through Arcadia, home to the 1930s **Santa Anita Park** (☏626-574-7223, tour info 626-574-6677; www.santaanita.com; 285 W Huntington Dr; tours free, race tickets $5-10, under 17yr free; ⏰racing Christmas–mid-Apr, late Sep-early Nov, tours 8.30am & 9.45am Sat & Sun). This track is where the Marx Brothers' *A Day at the Races* was filmed (and more recently the HBO series *Luck*) and where legendary thoroughbred Seabiscuit once ran. Stepping through the soaring art deco entrance into the grandstands, you'll feel like a million bucks – even if you don't win any wagers. During race season, tram tours go behind the scenes into the jockeys' room and training areas; reservations required. Continue along Colorado Blvd into wealthy **Old Pasadena**, a bustling 20-block shopping

ALAN COPSON / GETTY IMAGES ©

ALAN COPSON / GETTY IMAGES ©

WHY THIS IS A CLASSIC TRIP
NATE CAVALIERI, AUTHOR

Maybe it goes back to the transient vagabonds who founded this country, but there's a persistent call, deep in the American psyche, that compels us to hit the open road. And no road is quite as satisfying as the endless two-lane blacktop of Route 66. The subject of sing-alongs and fodder for daydreams, traveling this classic trail to the Pacific shore is an essentially American experience.

Top: Route 66 road marker
Left: Classic car detail
Right: Calico Ghost Town (p42)

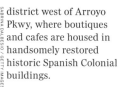

district west of Arroyo Pkwy, where boutiques and cafes are housed in handsomely restored historic Spanish Colonial buildings.

The Drive » Join the jet-set modern world on the Pasadena Fwy (Hwy 110), which streams south into LA. One of the first freeways in the US, it's a truck-free State Historic Freeway – the whole trip will take 20 minutes. If you're not quite ready for the trip to end, take a stroll through the glittering charms of LA.

⑩ Hollywood (p103)

Like a resurrected diva of the silver screen, **Hollywood** is making a comeback. Although it hasn't recaptured the Golden Age glamour that brought would-be starlets cruising here on Route 66, this historic neighborhood is still worth visiting for its restored movie palaces, unique museums and the pink stars on the **Walk of Fame**. The exact track Route 66 ran through the neighborhood isn't possible to follow these days (it changed officially a couple times and has long been paved over) but an exploration of the **Hollywood & Highland** (6801 Hollywood Blvd) complex, north of Santa Monica Blvd is a good place to get in the center of the action. The **Hollywood Visitor Information Center** (☏323-467-6412; www. discoverlosangeles.com;

⊙10am-10pm Mon-Sat, to 7pm Sun) is upstairs. Travelers looking for a fun, creepy communion with stars of yesteryear should stroll the **Hollywood Forever Cemetery** (www.hollywoodforever.com; 6000 Santa Monica Blvd; ⊙8am-5pm; P) next to Paramount Studios, which is crowded with famous 'immortals,' including Rudolph Valentino, Tyrone Power, Jayne Mansfield and Cecil B DeMille. Pick up a map ($5) at the flower shop near the entrance. They also offer **film screenings** here.

The Drive » Follow Santa Monica Blvd west for 11 miles to reach the end of the road – it makes a junction with the Pacific Coast Highway (Hwy 1). The pier is a few blocks to the south. Just north is Palisades Park.

TRIP HIGHLIGHT

11 Santa Monica (p100)

This is the end of the line: Route 66 reaches its

LOCAL KNOWLEDGE: AZTEC HOTEL

The **Aztec Hotel** (☎626-358-3231; 311 W Foothill Blvd, Monrovia) is just about as original as it can be. It's on the old alignment of Route 66. I never get tired of dropping by, and I always see something new here. The hotel is supposedly haunted by a lady who died here during her honeymoon. Historically, Hollywood celebrities would stop by the speakeasy before going to the races at Santa Anita Park.
Kevin Hansel, California Historic Route 66 Association

finish, over 2200 miles from its starting point in Chicago, on an ocean bluff in **Palisades Park**, where a Will Rogers Hwy memorial plaque marks the official end of the Mother Road. Celebrate on **Santa Monica Pier** (☎310-458-8900; www.santamonicapier.org; west of Ocean Ave; admission free; ⊙24hr; ♦♥), where you can ride a 1920s carousel featured in *The Sting*, gently touch tidepool critters at the **Santa Monica Pier Aquarium** (☎310-393-6149; www.

healthebay.org; 1600 Ocean Front Walk; adult/child $5/free; ⊙2-5pm Tue-Fri, 12:30-5pm Sat & Sun; ♦), and soak up a sunset atop the solar-powered Ferris wheel at **Pacific Park** (☎310-260-8744; www.pacpark.com; 380 Santa Monica Pier; unlimited rides over/under 42in tall $20/11; ⊙11am-9pm Sun-Thu, to midnight Fri & Sat Jun-Aug, shorter hours Sep-May; ♦). Year-round carnival rides include the West Coast's only oceanfront steel roller coaster – a thrilling ride to end this classic trip.

Right Santa Monica boardwalk

JAMES REEVE / GETTY IMAGES ©

Destinations

Eastern Route 66 (p50)
Start your nostalgic, kitschy adventure in downtown Chicago, before making your way through Illinois, Missouri, 13 miles of Kansas, and Oklahoma.

Central Route 66 (p70)
From Bryce Canyon to Wheeler Peak, eye-catching natural sites abound in the Southwest. And while these landmarks are stunning, it's often the journey between them that provides the memories.

Western Route 66 (p100)
Starting in hot, hot Needles on the Arizona border, speed through eerie ghost towns beside railroad tracks in the Mojave Desert, on to the waving palm trees and carnival pier of Santa Monica.

Native American performance, Gallup (p89)

Eastern Route 66

Get your big-city fix in Chicago before hitting the open road through the Great Plains.

ILLINOIS

Chicago dominates the state with its sky-high architecture and superlative museums, restaurants and music clubs. But venturing further afield reveals scattered shrines to local hero Abe Lincoln, and a trail of corn dogs, pies and drive-in movie theaters down Route 66.

❶ Resources

Illinois Bureau of Tourism (www.enjoyillinois.com)
Illinois Highway Conditions (www.gettingaroundillinois.com)
Illinois State Parks (www.dnr.illinois.gov/recreation) State parks are free to visit. Campsites cost $6 to $35.

Chicago

Loving Chicago is 'like loving a woman with a broken nose: you may well find lovelier lovelies, but never a lovely so real.' Writer Nelson Algren summed it up well in *Chicago: City on the Make*. There's something about this cloud-scraping city that bewitches. Well, maybe not during the six-month winter, when the 'Windy City' gets slapped by snowy blasts; however, come May, when the weather warms and everyone dashes for the outdoor festivals, ballparks, lakefront beaches and beer gardens – ah, nowhere tops Chicago (literally: some of the world's tallest buildings are here).

Beyond its mighty architecture, Chicago is a city of Mexican, Polish, Vietnamese and other ethnic neighborhoods in which to wander. It's a city of blues, jazz and rock clubs any night of the week. And it's a chowhound's town, where the queues for hot dogs equal the queues for reservations at North America's top restaurants.

Forgive us, but it has to be said: the Windy City will blow you away with its low-key, cultured awesomeness.

◉ Sights

Chicago's main attractions are found mostly in or near downtown.

The Loop – aka the city center and financial district – is named for the elevated train tracks that lasso its streets. It's busy all day, though not much happens at night other than in Millennium Park and the Theater District, near the intersection of N State and W Randolph Sts. The South Loop, which includes the lower ends of downtown and Grant Park, bustles with the lakefront Museum Campus and gleaming new residential high-rises.

Shops, restaurants and amusements abound in the Near North, while the Gold Coast has been the address of Chicago's wealthiest residents for over 125 years.

Willis Tower
Tower

(☎ 312-875-9696; www.the-skydeck.com; 233 S Wacker Dr; adult/child $19/12; ⊙ 9am-10pm Apr-Sep, 10am-8pm Oct-Mar; Ⓜ Brown, Orange, Purple, Pink Line to Quincy) It's Chicago's tallest building, and the 103rd-floor Skydeck puts you 1353ft into the heavens. Take the ear-popping, 70-second elevator ride to the top, then step onto one of the glass-floored ledges jutting mid-air for a knee-buckling perspective straight down. The entrance is on Jackson Blvd.

Shedd Aquarium
Aquarium

(☎ 312-939-2438; www.sheddaquarium.org; 1200 S Lake Shore Dr; adult/child $31/22; ⊙ 9am-5pm Mon-Fri, to 6pm Sat & Sun Sep-May, to 6pm daily Jun-Aug; ⊕; ☐ 146, 130) Top draws at the kiddie-mobbed Shedd Aquarium include the Oceanarium, with its beluga whales and frolicking white-sided dolphins, and the shark exhibit, where there's just 5in of Plexiglas between you and two dozen fierce-looking swimmers. The 4D theater, touch tanks and aquatic show cost extra (around $5 each).

Field Museum of Natural History
Museum

(☎ 312-922-9410; www.fieldmuseum.org; 1400 S Lake Shore Dr; adult/child $18/13; ⊙ 9am-5pm; ⊕; ☐ 146, 130) The mammoth Field Museum houses everything but the kitchen sink – beetles, mummies, gemstones, Bushman the stuffed ape... The collection's rock star is Sue, the largest *Tyrannosaurus rex* yet discovered. She even gets her own gift shop. Special exhibits and 3D movies cost extra.

Navy Pier
Waterfront

(☎ 312-595-7437; www.navypier.com; 600 E Grand Ave; ⊙ 10am-10pm Sun-Thu, to midnight Fri & Sat Jun-Aug, 10am-8pm Sun-Thu, to 10pm Fri & Sat Sep-May; ⊕; Ⓜ Red Line to Grand, then trolley) **FREE** Half-mile-long Navy Pier is Chicago's most-visited attraction, sporting a 150ft Ferris wheel and other carnival rides ($6 to $7 each), an IMAX theater, a beer garden, several boat-cruise operators and gimmicky chain restaurants. Locals groan over its commercialization, but its lakefront view and cool breezes can't be beat. The fireworks displays on summer Wednesdays (9:30pm) and Saturdays (10:15pm) are a treat too. A renovation is bringing an ice rink and additional amusements by 2016.

👉 Tours

Many companies offer discounts if you book online. Outdoor-oriented tours operate from April to November only, unless otherwise specified.

Chicago Architecture Foundation
Boat, Walking Tours

(CAF; ☎ 312-922-3432; www.architecture.org; 224 S Michigan Ave; tours $15-45; Ⓜ Brown, Orange, Green, Purple, Pink Line to Adams) The gold-standard boat tours ($42) sail from Michigan Ave's river dock. The popular Rise of the Skyscraper walking tours ($20) leave from the downtown Michigan Ave address. Weekday lunch-

Chicago skyline from Navy Pier

ALLAN BAXTER / GETTY IMAGES ©

Downtown Chicago

Alinea (1mi):
Steppenwolf
Theatre (1mi)

Old Town Ale House (0.8mi):
Second City (0.9mi)

25

E Pearson St

Chicago

Chicago

E Chicago Ave

W Chicago Ave

15

14

Ruxbin
(1.0mi)

W Superior St

NEAR
NORTH

24

W Huron St

19

W Erie St

W Ontario St

N Michigan Ave
(Magnificent Mile)

N Rush St

N Wabash Ave

W Ohio St

9

21

Quimby's (2.1mi)

W Grand Ave

22

Grand

Grand

W Grand Ave

N Milwaukee
Ave

N Orleans St

W Illinois St

17

30

23

13

N Dearborn St

N Clark St

W Hubbard St

N State St

E Kinzie St

Chicago
Architecture
Foundation
Boat Tour
Dock

W Kinzie St

W Kinzie St

North Branch Chicago River

Merchandise
Mart

W Wacker Dr

E Wacker Pl

ILLINOIS
CENTER

W Fulton St

WEST
LOOP

W Lake St

W Lake St

Clark Lake

E Lake
St

Chicago Cultural
Center Visitors
Center

16

Clinton

N Franklin St

N Wells St

Randolph

W Randolph St

Daley
Plaza

28

8

Millennium Park
Welcome Center

29

W Washington St

W Washington St

Washington

N Green St

N Halsted St

N Clinton St

N Desplaines St

12

Nichols
Bridgeway

Richard B Ogilvie
Transportation
Center (Metra)

THE
LOOP

Madison

20

W Madison St

Monroe

W Monroe St

W Monroe St

E Monroe St

Dan Ryan Expwy

W Marble Pl

Adams

18

W Adams St

Union
Station

5

Jackson

27

7

Quincy

S Green St

S Halsted St

S Desplaines St

S Wacker Dr

W Jackson Blvd

Megabus

LaSalle

Van Buren
St Station
(Metra)

W Van Buren St

W Van Buren St

Library

11

Clinton

LaSalle
St Station
(Metra)

10

E Congress Pkwy

UIC-
Halsted

Greyhound

LaSalle

W Harrison St

Harrison

Grant
Park

S Clinton St

S Canal St

South Branch Chicago River

S Wells St

S Financial Pl

S Clark St

S Federal St

E Balbo Ave

W Polk St

26

S Holden Ct

PRINTER'S
ROW

Tennis
Courts Dr

W Cabrini St

W 9th St

E 9th St

S Desplaines St

W Taylor St

E 11th St

DEARBORN
PARK

S Michigan Ave

Grant
Park

S Columbus Dr

Roosevelt

S Halsted St

90
94

W Roosevelt Rd

E Roosevelt Rd

Roosevelt
Rd/Museum
Campus Station

290

S Clark St

S Federal St

S State St

S Wabash Ave

CENTRAL
STATION

E 14th St

W 14th Pl

Downtown Chicago

◉ Sights

1	Field Museum of Natural History	E7
2	Millennium Park	D4
3	Navy Pier	F2
4	Shedd Aquarium	E6
5	Willis Tower	B4

✈ Activities & Tours

6	Bike Chicago	D3
7	Chicago Architecture Foundation	D4
8	Chicago Greeter	D3

🛏 Sleeping

9	Acme Hotel	C2
10	Buckingham Athletic Club Hotel	C5
11	HI-Chicago	D5
12	Hotel Burnham	C4

✗ Eating

13	Billy Goat Tavern	D2
14	Gino's East	D1
15	Giordano's	D1
16	Little Goat	A3
17	Lou Malnati's	C2
18	Lou Mitchell's	B4
19	Mr Beef	B1
20	Pizano's	D4
21	Pizzeria Uno	D2
22	Purple Pig	D2
23	Xoco	C2

🍷 Drinking & Nightlife

24	Clark Street Ale House	C1
25	Signature Lounge	D1

★ Entertainment

26	Buddy Guy's Legends	D5
27	Chicago Symphony Orchestra	D4
28	Goodman Theatre	C3
29	Grant Park Orchestra	D3

🛍 Shopping

	Chicago Architecture Foundation Shop	see 7
30	Jazz Record Mart	D2

time tours ($15) explore individual landmark buildings. Buy tickets online or at CAF.

Chicago Greeter   Walking Tour

(www.chicagogreeter.com) FREE Get paired with a local city dweller who will take you on a personal two- to four-hour tour customized by theme (architecture, history, gay and lesbian, and more) or neighborhood. Travel is by foot and/or public transportation. Reserve 10 business days in advance.

Bike Chicago _Cycling_

(☑ 312-729-1000; www.bikechicago.com; 239 E Randolph St; bikes per hr/day from $9/36, tour adult/ child from $40/30; ⊙ 6:30am-7pm Mon-Fri year-round, from 9am Sat & Sun Apr-Oct; Ⓜ Brown, Orange, Green, Purple, Pink Line to Randolph) Rent a bike to explore DIY-style, or go on a guided tour. The latter cover themes such as lakefront parks and attractions, pizza and hot-dog munching, or downtown's sights and fireworks at night (highly recommended). Prices include lock, helmet and map.

🛏 Sleeping

Hotels in the Loop are convenient to the museums, festival grounds and business district, but the area is pretty dead come nightfall. Accommodations in the Near North and Gold Coast are most popular, given their proximity to eating, shopping and entertainment venues.

Wi-fi is free unless noted otherwise. You pay dearly for parking in Chicago; around $50 per night downtown, and $22 in outlying neighborhoods.

HI-Chicago _Hostel $_

(☑ 312-360-0300; www.hichicago.org; 24 E Congress Pkwy; dm incl breakfast $32-40; Ⓟ ❋ @ 🛜; Ⓜ Brown, Orange, Purple, Pink Line to Library) Chicago's best hostel is immaculate, conveniently placed in the Loop, and offers bonuses such as a staffed information desk, free volunteer-led tours and discount passes to museums and shows. The simple dorm rooms have six to 12 beds, and most have attached baths.

Buckingham Athletic Club Hotel _Boutique Hotel $$_

(☑ 312-663-8910; www.bac-chicago.com; 440 S LaSalle St; r incl breakfast $179-249; Ⓟ ❋ 🛜 🏊; Ⓜ Brown, Orange, Purple, Pink Line to LaSalle) Tucked into the 40th floor of the Chicago Stock Exchange building, this 21-room hotel is not easy to find. The benefit if you do? Rooms so spacious they'd be considered suites elsewhere. There's also free access to the namesake gym with lap pool.

Acme Hotel _Boutique Hotel $$$_

(☑ 312-894-0800; www.acmehotelcompany.com; 15 E Ohio St; r $179-309; Ⓟ ❋ @ 🛜; Ⓜ Red Line to Grand) Urban bohemians love the Acme for its indie-cool style at (usually) affordable rates. The 130 rooms mix industrial fixtures with retro lamps, mid-century furniture and funky modern art. They're wired up with free wi-fi, good speakers, smart TVs and easy connections to stream your own music and movies. Graffiti, neon and lava lights decorate the common areas.

Hotel Burnham _Boutique Hotel $$$_

(☑ 312-782-1111; www.burnhamhotel.com; 1 W Washington St; r $269-399; Ⓟ ❋ @ 🛜 🏊; Ⓜ Blue Line to Washington) The proprietors brag that the Burnham has the highest guest return rates in Chicago; it's easy to see why. Housed in the landmark 1890s Reliance Building (a precedent for the modern skyscraper), its slick decor woos architecture buffs. Mahogany writing desks and chaise longues furnish the bright, butter-colored rooms. A free wine happy hour takes place each evening.

🍴 Eating

Need help deciding where to eat? LTH Forum (www.lthforum.com) is a great local resource.

The Loop & West Loop

Most Loop eateries are geared towards lunch crowds of office workers. The West Loop booms with hot-chef restaurants.

Lou Mitchell's _Breakfast $_

See p18.

Little Goat _Diner $$_

(www.littlegoatchicago.com; 820 W Randolph St; mains $8-14; ⊙ 7am-10pm Sun-Thu, to midnight Fri & Sat; 🛜 🍽; Ⓜ Green, Pink Line to Morgan) _Top Chef_ winner Stephanie Izard opened this diner for the foodie masses across the street from her ever-booked main restaurant, Girl and the Goat. Sit on a vintage twirly stool and order off the all-day breakfast menu. Better yet, try lunchtime favorites like the goat sloppy joe with mashed potato tempura or the pork belly on scallion pancakes.

Near North

This is where you'll find Chicago's mother lode of restaurants.

Billy Goat Tavern _Burgers $_

(www.billygoattavern.com; lower level, 430 N Michigan Ave; burgers $4-6; ⊙ 6am-2am Mon-Fri, 10am-2am Sat & Sun; Ⓜ Red Line to Grand) _Tribune_ and _Sun-Times_ reporters have guzzled in the subterranean Billy Goat for decades. Order a 'cheezborger' and Schlitz, then look around at the newspapered walls to get the scoop on infamous local stories, such as the Cubs Curse.

Xoco
Mexican $$

(www.rickbayless.com; 449 N Clark St; mains $8-13; ⊗8am-9pm Tue-Thu, to 10pm Fri & Sat; M Red Line to Grand) ✐ Crunch into warm *churros* for breakfast, meaty *tortas* (sandwiches) for lunch and rich *caldos* (soups) for dinner at celeb chef Rick Bayless' Mexican street-food joint.

Purple Pig
Mediterranean $$

(☑312-464-1744; www.thepurplepigchicago.com; 500 N Michigan Ave; small plates $8-16; ⊗11:30am-midnight Sun-Thu, to 1am Fri & Sat; ☑; M Red Line to Grand) The Pig's Magnificent Mile location, wide-ranging meat and veggie menu, long list of affordable vinos and late-night serving hours make it a crowd-pleaser. Milk-braised pork shoulder is the hamtastic specialty.

Lincoln Park & Lake View

Halsted and Clark Sts are the main veins teeming with restaurants and bars.

Crisp
Asian $

(www.crisponline.com; 2940 N Broadway; mains $8-12; ⊗11:30am-9pm; M Brown Line to Wellington) Music pours from the stereo, and cheap, delicious Korean fusions arrive from the kitchen at this cheerful cafe. The 'Bad Boy Buddha' bowl, a variation on *bi bim bop* (mixed vegetables with rice), is one of the best cheap lunches in town.

Alinea
Modern American $$$

(☑312-867-0110; www.alinearestaurant.com; 1723 N Halsted St; multicourse menu $210-265; ⊗5-9:30pm Wed-Sun; M Red Line to North/Clybourn) Widely regarded as North America's best restaurant, Alinea brings on 18 to 22 courses of mind-bending molecular gastronomy. There are no reservations; instead, Alinea sells tickets two to three months in advance. Sign up at the website for details and check the Twitter feed (@Alinea) for possible last-minute seats.

Wicker Park, Bucktown & Ukrainian Village

Trendy restaurants open almost every day in these 'hoods.

Irazu
Latin American $$

(☑773-252-5687; www.irazuchicago.com; 1865 N Milwaukee Ave; mains $9-14; ⊗11:30am-9:30pm Mon-Sat; M Blue Line to Western) Chicago's unassuming lone Costa Rican eatery turns out

---

CHICAGO'S HOLY TRINITY OF SPECIALTIES

Chicago cooks up three beloved specialties. Foremost is **deep-dish pizza**, a hulking mass of crust that rises two or three inches above the plate and cradles a molten pile of toppings. One gooey piece is practically a meal. A large pizza averages $22 at the following places:

Pizzeria Uno (www.unos.com; 29 E Ohio St; small pizzas from $13; ⊗11am-1am Mon-Fri, to 2am Sat, to 11pm Sun; M Red Line to Grand) The deep-dish concept supposedly originated here in 1943.

Gino's East (www.ginoseast.com; 162 E Superior St; small pizzas from $15; ⊗11am-9:30pm Mon-Sat, from noon Sun; M Red Line to Chicago) Write on the walls while you wait for your pie.

Lou Malnati's (www.loumalnatis.com; 439 N Wells St; small pizzas from $12; ⊗11am-11pm Sun-Thu, to midnight Fri & Sat; M Brown, Purple Line to Merchandise Mart) Famous for its butter crust.

Giordano's (www.giordanos.com; 730 N Rush St; small pizzas from $15.50; ⊗11am-11pm Sun-Thu, to midnight Fri & Sat; M Red Line to Chicago) Perfectly tangy tomato sauce.

Pizano's (www.pizanoschicago.com; 864 N State St; 10in pizzas from $14; ⊗11am-2am Sun-Fri, to 3am Sat; M Red Line to Chicago) Oprah's favorite.

No less iconic is the Chicago hot dog – a wiener that's been 'dragged through the garden' (ie topped with onions, tomatoes, shredded lettuce, bell peppers, pepperoncini and sweet relish, or variations thereof, but *never* ketchup), and then cushioned on a poppyseed bun. Portillo's (☑312-587-8910; www.portillos.com; 100 W Ontario St; mains $4-7; ⊗10am-1pm Sun-Thu, to midnight Fri & Sat; M Red Line to Grand) stacks a nice one.

The city is also revered for its spicy, drippy, only-in-Chicago **Italian beef sandwiches**. Mr Beef (666 N Orleans St; sandwiches $4-7; ⊗9am-5pm Mon-Fri, 10am-3pm Sat, plus 10:30pm-4am Fri & Sat; M Brown, Purple Line to Chicago) serves the gold standard.

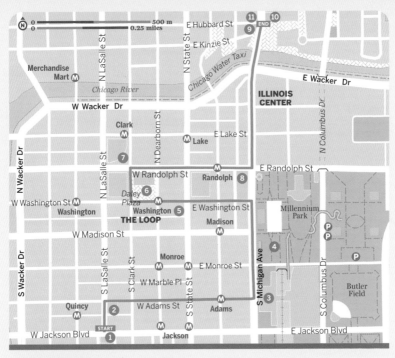

City Walk
The Loop

START: CHICAGO BOARD OF TRADE
END: BILLY GOAT TAVERN
LENGTH: 3 MILES; 2 HOURS

This tour swoops through the Loop, highlighting Chicago's revered art and architecture, with a visit to Al Capone's dentist thrown in for good measure.

Start at the ① **Chicago Board of Trade**, where guys in Technicolor coats swap corn (or something like that) inside a cool art-deco building. Step into the nearby ② **Rookery** to see Frank Lloyd Wright's handiwork in the atrium.

Head east on Adams St to the ③ **Art Institute**, one of the city's most-visited attractions. The lion statues out front make a classic keepsake photo. Walk a few blocks north to avant-garde ④ **Millennium Park**.

Leave the park and head west on Washington St to ⑤ **Hotel Burnham**. It's housed in the Reliance Building, which was the precursor to modern skyscraper design;

Capone's dentist drilled teeth in what's now room 809. Just west, Picasso's abstract ⑥ **Untitled** sculpture is ensconced in Daley Plaza. Baboon, dog, woman? You decide. Then go north on Clark St to Jean Dubuffet's ⑦ **Monument with Standing Beast**, another head-scratching sculpture.

Walk east on Randolph St through the theater district. Pop into the ⑧ **Chicago Cultural Center** to see what free art exhibits or concerts are on. Now go north on Michigan Ave and cross the Chicago River. Just north of the bridge you'll pass the ⑨ **Wrigley Building**, shining bright and white, and the nearby Gothic, eye-popping ⑩ **Tribune Tower**.

To finish your tour, visit ⑪ **Billy Goat Tavern**, a vintage Chicago dive that spawned the Curse of the Cubs after the tavern's owner, Billy Sianis, tried to enter Wrigley Field with his pet goat. The smelly creature was denied entry, so Sianis called down a mighty curse on the baseball team in retaliation. They've stunk ever since.

burritos bursting with chicken, black beans and fresh avocado, and sandwiches dressed in a heavenly, spicy-sweet vegetable sauce. Wash them down with an *avena* (a slurpable oatmeal milkshake). Cash only.

Ruxbin
Modern American $$$

(📞 312-624-8509; www.ruxbinchicago.com; 851 N Ashland Ave; mains $26-32; ⊙ 6-10pm Tue-Fri, 5:30-10pm Sat, 5:30-9pm Sun; Ⓜ Blue Line to Division) 🍴 The passion of the brother-sister team who run Ruxbin is evident in everything from the warm decor made of found items to the artfully prepared flavors in dishes like the pork-belly salad with grapefruit, cornbread and blue cheese. It's a wee place of just 32 seats, and it's BYO.

Logan Square

Logan Sq has become a mecca for inventive, no-pretense chefs. Eats and drinks ring the intersection of Milwaukee, Logan and Kedzie Blvds.

Longman & Eagle
American $$$

(📞 773-276-7110; www.longmanandeagle.com; 2657 N Kedzie Ave; mains $15-30; ⊙ 9am-2am Sun-Fri, to 3am Sat; Ⓜ Blue Line to Logan Sq) Hard to say whether this shabby-chic tavern is best for eating or drinking. Let's say eating, since it earned a Michelin star for its beautifully cooked comfort foods such as vanilla brioche French toast for breakfast, wild-boar sloppy joes for lunch and maple-braised pork shank for dinner. There's a whole menu of juicy small plates, too. Reservations not accepted.

🍷 Drinking & Nightlife

Signature Lounge
Lounge

(www.signatureroom.com; 875 N Michigan Ave; drinks $6-16; ⊙ 11am-12:30am Sun-Thu, to 1:30am Fri & Sat; Ⓜ Red Line to Chicago) Grab the elevator up to the 96th floor of the John Hancock Center (Chicago's third-tallest skyscraper) and order a beverage while looking out over the city. Women: don't miss the bathroom view.

Clark Street Ale House
Bar

(www.clarkstreetalehouse.com; 742 N Clark St; ⊙ 4pm-4am Mon-Fri, 11am-5am Sat, 11am-4am Sun; Ⓜ Red Line to Chicago) Do as the retro sign advises and 'Stop & Drink Liquor.' Midwestern microbrews are the main draw; order a three-beer sampler for $7. When the weather warms, a sweet beer garden beckons out back.

Old Town Ale House
Bar

(www.theoldtownalehouse.com; 219 W North Ave; ⊙ 3pm-4am Mon-Fri, noon-5am Sat, noon-4am Sun; Ⓜ Brown, Purple Line to Sedgwick) This unpretentious favorite lets you mingle with beautiful people and grizzled regulars, seated pint by pint under the nude-politician paintings. It's across the street from Second City.

Gingerman Tavern
Bar

(3740 N Clark St; ⊙ 3pm-2am Mon-Fri, noon-3am Sat, noon-2am Sun; Ⓜ Red Line to Addison) The pool tables, good beer selection and pierced-and-tattooed patrons make Gingerman wonderfully different from the surrounding Wrigleyville sports bars.

☆ Entertainment

Check www.chicagoreader.com for listings.

Green Mill
Jazz

(www.greenmilljazz.com; 4802 N Broadway; cover charge $5-15; ⊙ noon-4am Mon-Sat, from 11am Sun; Ⓜ Red Line to Lawrence) The timeless Green Mill earned its notoriety as Al Capone's favorite speakeasy (the tunnels where he hid the booze are still underneath the bar). Sit in one of the curved leather booths and feel his ghost urging you on to another martini. Local and national jazz artists perform nightly; Green Mill also hosts the nationally acclaimed poetry slam on Sundays.

HOW TO FIND A REAL CHICAGO BAR

Unfortunately, we can't list every watering hole in town, but we can give you the tools to go out and discover classic, character-filled bars on your own. Look for the following:

» an 'Old Style' beer sign swinging out front

» a well-worn dart board and/or pool table inside

» patrons wearing ballcaps with the logo of the Cubs, White Sox or Bears

» bottles of brew served in buckets of ice

» sports on TV.

Buddy Guy's Legends · Blues

(www.buddyguy.com; 700 S Wabash Ave; tickets Sun-Thu $10, Fri & Sat $20; ⊙5pm-2am Mon & Tue, 11am-2am Wed-Fri, noon-3am Sat, noon-2am Sun; Ⓜ Red Line to Harrison) Top local and national acts wail on the stage of local icon Buddy Guy. The man himself usually plugs in his axe for a series of shows in January. The venue hosts free, all-ages acoustic performances from noon to 2pm Wednesday through Sunday.

Hideout · Live Music

(www.hideoutchicago.com; 1354 W Wabansia Ave; ⊙7pm-2am Tue, 4pm-2am Wed-Fri, 7pm-3am Sat, varies Sun & Mon; 📷72) Hidden behind a factory at the edge of Bucktown, this two-room lodge of indie rock and alt-country is well worth seeking out. The owners have nursed an outsider, underground vibe, and the place feels like the downstairs of your grandma's rumpus room. Music and other events (bingo, literary readings etc) take place nightly.

Metro · Live Music

(www.metrochicago.com; 3730 N Clark St; Ⓜ Red Line to Addison) Local bands on the verge of stardom and national names looking for an 'intimate' venue turn up the volume at Metro.

Grant Park Orchestra · Classical Music

(☑312-742-7638; www.grantparkmusicfestival.com; Pritzker Pavilion, Millennium Park; ⊙6:30pm Wed & Fri, 7:30pm Sat mid-Jun–mid-Aug; Ⓜ Brown, Orange, Green, Purple, Pink Line to Randolph) FREE The beloved group puts on free classical concerts in Millennium Park throughout the summer.

Chicago Symphony Orchestra · Classical Music

(☑312-294-3000; www.cso.org; 220 S Michigan Ave; Ⓜ Brown, Orange, Green, Purple, Pink Line to Adams) One of America's best symphonies plays in the Daniel Burnham–designed Orchestra Hall.

Theater & Comedy

Chicago's reputation for stage drama is well deserved; many productions export to Broadway. The Theater District is a cluster of big, neon-lit venues at State and Randolph Sts. Broadway in Chicago (☑800-775-2000; www.broadwayinchicago.com) handles tickets for most.

Improv comedy began in Chicago, and the city still nurtures the best in the business.

Steppenwolf Theatre · Theater

(☑312-335-1650; www.steppenwolf.org; 1650 N Halsted St; Ⓜ Red Line to North/Clybourn) Drama club of Malkovich, Sinise and other Hollywood stars; 2 miles north of the Loop in Lincoln Park.

DISCOUNT TICKETS

For same-week theater seats at half price, try Hot Tix. You can buy them online (www.hottix.org) or in person at the three downtown booths. The selection is best early in the week.

Goodman Theatre · Theater

(☑312-443-3800; www.goodmantheatre.org; 170 N Dearborn St; Ⓜ Brown, Orange, Green, Purple, Pink, Blue Line to Clark/Lake) The city's other powerhouse, known for new and classic American works.

Second City · Comedy

(☑312-337-3992; www.secondcity.com; 1616 N Wells St; Ⓜ Brown, Purple Line to Sedgwick) It's the cream of the crop, where Bill Murray, Stephen Colbert, Tina Fey and many more honed their wit. Bargain: turn up after the evening's last show (Friday excluded) and watch the comics improv a performance for free.

iO Theater · Comedy

(☑312-929-2401; ioimprov.com/chicago; 1501 N Kingsbury St; Ⓜ Red Line to North/Clybourn) Chicago's other major improv house, with four stages hosting bawdy shows nightly.

Sports
Chicago Cubs · Baseball

(www.cubs.com; 1060 W Addison St; Ⓜ Red Line to Addison) The Cubs last won the World Series in 1908, but that doesn't stop fans from coming out to see them. Part of the draw is atmospheric, ivy-walled Wrigley Field, which dates from 1914. The raucous bleacher seats are the most popular place to sit. No tickets? Peep through the 'knothole,' a garage-door-size opening on Sheffield Ave.

Chicago White Sox · Baseball

(www.whitesox.com; 333 W 35th St; Ⓜ Red Line to Sox-35th) The Sox are the Cubs' South Side rivals and play in the more modern 'Cell,' aka US Cellular Field. Tickets are usually cheaper than at Wrigley Field; Monday is half-price night.

🛍 Shopping

A siren song for shoppers emanates from N Michigan Ave, along the Magnificent Mile.

Chicago Architecture Foundation
Shop
Souvenirs

(www.architecture.org/shop; 224 S Michigan Ave; ⊙9am-6:30pm; Ⓜ Brown, Orange, Green, Purple, Pink Line to Adams) Skyline posters, Frank Lloyd Wright note cards, skyscraper models and more for those with an edifice complex.

Strange Cargo
Clothing

(www.strangecargo.com; 3448 N Clark St; ⊙11am-6:45pm Mon-Sat, to 5:30pm Sun; Ⓜ Red Line to Addison) This retro store stocks kitschy iron-on T-shirts featuring Ditka, Obama and other renowned Chicagoans.

Jazz Record Mart
Music

(www.jazzmart.com; 27 E Illinois St; ⊙10am-7pm Mon-Sat, noon-5pm Sun; Ⓜ Red Line to Grand) One-stop shop for Chicago jazz and blues CDs and vinyl.

Quimby's
Books

(www.quimbys.com; 1854 W North Ave; ⊙noon-9pm Mon-Thu, to 10pm Fri & Sat, to 7pm Sun; Ⓜ Blue Line to Damen) Ground Zero for comics, 'zines and underground culture; in Wicker Park.

ⓘ Information

TOURIST INFORMATION
Chicago Cultural Center Visitors Center
(www.choosechicago.com; 77 E Randolph St; ⊙10am-5pm Mon-Sat, 11am-4pm Sun; 🛜; Ⓜ Brown, Orange, Green, Purple, Pink Line to Randolph) There's a staffed information desk, CTA transit-card kiosk and free wi-fi. Free Ins-

taGreeter (Friday through Sunday year-round) and Millennium Park (daily mid-May to mid-October) tours also depart from here.

WEBSITES
Chicagoist (www.chicagoist.com) Quirky take on food, arts and events.

Gapers Block (www.gapersblock.com) News and events site with Chicago attitude.

Huffington Post Chicago (www.huffingtonpost.com/chicago) Amalgamates news from major local sources.

ⓘ Getting Around

Be warned: street and garage/lot parking is expensive. If you must, try **Millennium Park Garage** (www.millenniumgarages.com; 5 S Columbus Dr; per 3/24hr $23/30). Chicago's rush-hour traffic is abysmal.

Springfield

The small state capital has a serious obsession with Abraham Lincoln, who practiced law here from 1837 to 1861. Many of the attractions are walkable downtown and cost little or nothing.

Old State Capitol
Historic Site

(📞 217-785-7960; cnr 6th & Adams Sts; ⊙9am-5pm, closed Sun-Tue Sep-May) Chatterbox docents will take you through the building and regale you with Lincoln stories, such as how he gave his famous 'House Divided' speech here in 1858. Suggested donation is $4.

N Michigan Ave, Chicago's foremost shopping strip

Statehouse Inn
Hotel $$

(☑ 217-528-5100; www.thestatehouseinn.com; 101 E Adams St; r incl breakfast $115-155; P ❋ @ 🛜) It looks concrete-drab outside, but inside shows its style. Comfy beds and large baths fill the rooms; a retro bar fills the lobby.

Inn at 835
B&B $$

(☑ 217-523-4466; www.innat835.com; 835 S 2nd St; r incl breakfast $130-200; P ❋ 🛜) The historic, arts and crafts–style manor offers 11 rooms of the four-post bed, claw-foot bathtub variety.

Norb Andy's Tabarin
Pub Food $

(www.norbandys.com; 518 E Capitol Ave; mains $7-10; ⊘ 11am-1am Tue-Fri, 4pm-1am Sat) A favorite with locals, Norb's is a dive-bar-restaurant housed in the 1837 Hickox House downtown. It piles up Springfield's best 'horseshoe,' a local sandwich of fried meat on toasted bread, mounded with french fries and smothered in melted cheese.

Route 66 Drive In
Cinema

(☑ 217-698-0066; www.route66-drivein.com; 1700 Recreation Dr; adult/child $7/4; ⊘ nightly Jun-Aug, weekends mid-Apr–May & Sep) Screens first-run flicks under the stars.

Springfield Convention & Visitors Bureau
Tourist Information

(www.visitspringfieldillinois.com) Produces a useful visitors' guide.

MISSOURI

The most populated state in the Plains, Missouri likes to mix things up, serving visitors ample portions of both sophisticated city life and down-home country sights. St Louis and Kansas City are the region's most interesting cities and each is a destination in its own right. But, with more forest and less farm field than neighboring states, Missouri also cradles plenty of wild places and wide-open spaces, most notably the rolling Ozark Mountains, where the winding valleys invite adventurous exploring or just some laid-back meandering behind the steering wheel.

ℹ️ Information

Bed & Breakfast Inns, Missouri (www.bbim.org)
Missouri Division of Tourism (www.visitmo.com)
Missouri State Parks (www.mostateparks.com) State parks are free to visit. Site fees range from $13 to $28 and some sites may be reserved in advance.

St Louis

Slide into St Louis and revel in the vibe of the largest city in the Great Plains. Beer, bowling and baseball are some of the top attractions, but history and culture, much of it linked to the Mississippi River, are a vital part of the fabric. And, of course, there's the iconic Gateway Arch that you have seen in a million pictures, but which is even more impressive in reality. Many music legends, including Scott Joplin, Chuck Berry, Tina Turner and Miles Davis got their start here and the bouncy live-music venues keep the flame burning.

◎ Sights & Activities

The landmark Gateway Arch (see p20) rises right along the Mississippi River. Begin a visit downtown, which runs west of the arch, and wander for half a day. Then explore the rest of the city. The neighborhoods of most interest radiate from this core, including the following:

➜ **Central West End** Just east of Forest Park, a posh center for nightlife and shopping.

➜ **The Hill** An Italian-American neighborhood with good delis and eateries.

➜ **Lafayette Square** Historic, upscale and trendy.

➜ **The Loop** Northwest of Forest Park, funky shops and nightlife line Delmar Blvd.

➜ **Soulard** The city's oldest quarter, with good cafes, bars and blues.

➜ **South Grand** Bohemian and gentrifying, this area surrounds beautiful Tower Grove Park and has a slew of ethnic restaurants.

Cross the river to see Cahokia Mounds State Historic Site (☑ 618-346-5160; www.cahokiamounds.org; Collinsville Rd; suggested donation adult/child $7/2; ⊘ grounds 8am-dusk year-round, visitor center 9am-5pm, closed Mon & Tue Sep-May).

City Museum
Museum

(www.citymuseum.org; 701 N 15th St; admission $12, Ferris wheel $5; ⊘ 9am-5pm Wed & Thu, 9am-midnight Fri & Sat, 11am-5pm Sun; ♿) Possibly the wildest highlight of any visit to St Louis is this frivolous, frilly fun house in a vast old shoe factory. Run, jump and explore all manner of exhibits. An aquarium, circus

Downtown St Louis

performers and the World's Largest Underwear are among the marvels. The summer-only rooftop Ferris wheel offers grand views of the city.

Forest Park
Park, Museum

(www.forestparkforever.org; ☉6am-10pm) New York City may have Central Park, but St Louis has the bigger (by 528 acres) Forest Park. The superb, 1371-acre spread was the setting of the 1904 World's Fair. It's a beautiful place to escape to and is dotted with attractions, many free. Two walkable neighborhoods, The Loop and Central West End, are close.

The Visitor and Education Center (5595 Grand Dr; ☉6am-8pm) is in an old streetcar pavilion and has a cafe. Free walking tours leave from here and you can borrow an iPod audio tour.

Missouri History Museum
Museum

(www.mohistory.org; 5700 Lindell Blvd; ☉10am-5pm, to 8pm Tue) FREE Presents the story of St Louis, starring such worthies as the World's Fair, Charles Lindbergh (look for the sales receipt for his first plane – he bought it at a variety store!) and a host of blues performers. Oral histories from those who fought segregation are moving.

Downtown St Louis

◎ Sights
1   City Museum.........................B1
2   Jefferson National Expansion
    Memorial/Gateway Arch............D2
3   Old Courthouse & Museum..........C2

🍷 Drinking & Nightlife
4   Blueberry Hill......................B2
5   Bridge Tap House & Wine Bar........C2

★ Entertainment
6   Busch Stadium.....................C2

St Louis Art Museum
Museum

(www.slam.org; 1 Fine Arts Dr; ☉10am-5pm Tue-Thu, Sat & Sun, to 9pm Fri) FREE A grand beaux-arts palace originally built for the World's Fair. Now housing this storied institution, its collections span time and styles. A stunning new wing opened in 2013.

St Louis Zoo
Zoo

(www.stlzoo.org; 1 Government Dr; fee for some exhibits; ☉9am-5pm daily, to 7pm Fri-Sun Jun-Aug; 👶) FREE Divided into themed zones, this vast zoo includes a fascinating River's Edge area with African critters.

Forest Park (p61), St Louis
FERGUSON & KATZMAN / GETTY IMAGES ©

St Louis Science Center
Museum

(www.slsc.org; 5050 Oakland Ave; ⊙9:30am-4:30pm Mon-Sat, 11am-4:30pm Sun Sep-May, to 5:30pm daily Jun-Aug; 🚼) **FREE** Live demonstrations, dinosaurs, a planetarium and an IMAX theater (additional fee).

🛏 Sleeping

Most midrange and upscale chains have a hotel near the Gateway Arch in downtown. Indie cheapies are thin on the ground in interesting areas but you'll find plenty near the airport and you can ride the MetroLink light-rail into the city. Upscale Clayton on I-170 (exit 1F) also has rail access and a cluster of chains.

Huckleberry Finn Hostel
Hostel $

(☑314-374-8696; www.huckfinnhostel.com; 1908 S 12th St; dm from $25; ❄) Occupying two old town houses, this independent hostel is basic, but it's a friendly gathering spot with a piano in the lounge/kitchen, and free lockers. Its Soulard location is ideal. Be sure to reserve ahead.

Parkway Hotel
Hotel $$

(☑314-256-7777; www.theparkwayhotel.com; 4550 Forest Park Ave; r $130-270; P❄@🛜🐾) Right in the midst of Central West End's upscale fun, this indie eight-story hotel contains 217 modern rooms inside a grand limestone building. Standards are high, hot breakfasts

are included and you can't beat the location right across from Forest Park.

Napoleon's Retreat
B&B $$

(☑314-772-6979; www.napoleonsretreat.com; 1815 Lafayette Ave; r $130-200; ❄@🛜) A lovely Second French Empire home in historic and leafy Lafayette Sq, this B&B has five bold and beautiful rooms, each with private bath and antique furnishings. There's a $20 surcharge for single-night stays.

Moonrise Hotel
Boutique Hotel $$

(☑314-721-1111; www.moonrisehotel.com; 6177 Delmar Blvd; r $130-260; P❄@🛜🐾) The stylish eight-story Moonrise has a high profile amid the high energy of the Loop neighborhood. The 125 rooms sport a lunar motif but are grounded enough to slow things down to comfy.

🍽 Eating

St Louis boasts the region's most diverse selection of food. The magazine and website *Sauce* (www.saucemagazine.com) is full of reviews.

Downtown & Midtown

Laclede's Landing, along the riverfront next to the historic Eads Railway Bridge, has several restaurants, though generally people pop down here for the atmosphere – cobblestoned streets, converted brick buildings and free-flowing beer – rather than the food.

Crown Candy Kitchen
Cafe $

(www.crowncandykitchen.net; 1401 St Louis Ave; mains $5-10; ⊙10:30am-8pm Mon-Thu, to 9pm Fri & Sat) An authentic family-run soda fountain that's been making families smile since 1913. Malts (try the butterscotch) come with spoons, the floats, well, float, and you can try the famous BLT. Homemade candies top it off. It's an oasis in the struggling North St Louis neighborhood.

Pappy's Smokehouse
Barbecue $$

(☑314-535-4340; www.pappyssmokehouse.com; 3106 Olive St; mains from $9; ⊙11am-7pm Mon-Sat, to 4pm Sun) Named one of the nation's best joints for barbecue, Pappy's serves luscious ribs, pulled pork, brisket and smoked turkey. With fame, however, comes popularity, so be prepared for long lines and crowded communal dining. Ameliorate the wait with dreams of the sweet-potato fries.

Soulard & Lafayette Square

Restaurants and pubs occupy most corners in Soulard, with plenty of live blues and Irish music. Just wander. Historic Lafayette Sq, 1 mile northwest, has various stylish spots.

Soulard Farmers Market   Market $

(www.soulardmarket.com; 730 Carroll St; ☺8am-5pm Wed & Thu, from 7am Fri & Sat) A local treasure with a range of vendors selling regional produce, baked goods and prepared foods. Picnic or nosh yourself silly. Dating to 1779, it's pretension-free.

Bogart's Smoke House   Barbecue $$

(www.bogartssmokehouse.com; 1627 S 9th St; mains $9-16; ☺10:30am-4pm Mon-Thu, to 8pm Fri & Sat) The soul of Soulard? The smoky meats here draw lines of people who tear into all the standards plus specialties like prime rib. Extras such as the searingly hot voodoo sauce and the 'fire and ice pickles' have creative flair.

South Grand

This young, bohemian area near beautiful Tower Grove Park has a slew of excellent multicultural restaurants, many with outside terraces.

MoKaBe's Coffeehouse   Cafe $

(3606 Arsenal St; mains $5-7; ☺8am-midnight; 🛜🖋) Overlooking Tower Grove Park, this hangout for hipsters and neighborhood activists (it was a hot spot during the 2014 Ferguson protests) buzzes day and night. Grab a coffee, a baked treat, breakfast or a sandwich and ponder the views.

The Hill

This Italian neighborhood crammed with cute little houses has innumerable pasta joints. Stroll the tidy streets and stop for a coffee at an Italian cafe or deli.

Mama Toscano's   Italian $

(www.mamatoscano.com; 2201 Macklind Ave; mains $5-8; ☺7am-6pm Tue-Fri, to 5pm Sat) More grocery than cafe, this corner Hill legend is renowned for its ravioli. Get an order toasted and enjoy outside at a picnic table (it's table-free inside). Other highlights include the sandwiches, especially the eggplant number; get it on garlic bread.

Milo's Bocce Garden   Italian $$

(www.milosboccegarden.com; 5201 Wilson Ave; mains $6-14; ☺11am-1am Mon-Sat) Enjoy sandwiches, pizzas and pastas in the vast outdoor courtyard or inside the old-world bar. Watch and join the regulars on the busy bocce ball courts.

Central West End & the Loop

Sidewalk cafes rule Euclid Ave in posh and trendy old Central West End. The Loop is near Washington University and runs along Delmar Blvd (embedded with the St Louis Walk of Fame); it has many bars and ethnic restaurants catering to a hipster crowd.

Pickles Deli   Deli $

(www.picklesdelistl.com; 22 N Euclid Ave; mains $5-10; ☺9am-7pm Mon-Fri, 10am-3pm Sat) Top ingredients separate this slick deli from humdrum sandwich chains; for example, the French dip is laden with house-roasted beef. Options include excellent avocado spread and much more. Dine in or picnic in Forest Park.

ST LOUIS SPECIALTIES

Frozen custard Don't dare leave town without licking yourself silly on this super-creamy ice-cream-like treat at historic Ted Drewes (p20), west of the city center. There's a smaller summer-only branch south of the city center at 4224 S Grand Blvd. Rich and poor rub elbows enjoying a 'concrete,' a delectable stirred-up combination of flavors.

Toasted ravioli They're filled with meat, coated in breadcrumbs, then deep-fried. Practically every restaurant on the Hill serves them, notably Mama Toscano's.

St Louis pizza Its thin-crusted, square-cut pizzas are really addictive. They're made with Provel cheese, a locally beloved gooey concoction of processed cheddar, Swiss and provolone. Local chain Imo's (www.imospizza.com; large from $16), with more than 70 locations across the metro area, bakes 'the square beyond compare.'

Boston Avenue United Methodist Church, Tulsa

🍷 Drinking & Nightlife

Schlafly, Civil Life and Urban Chestnut are excellent local microbrews that will let you forget that you're in the home of Bud. The website www.stlhops.com is an excellent guide to local beers and where to drink them.

Laclede's Landing, Soulard and the Loop are loaded with pubs and bars, many with live music. Most bars close at 1:30am, though some have 3am licenses.

Blueberry Hill   Bar
(www.blueberryhill.com; 6504 Delmar Blvd; ⊙ 11am-late) St Louis native Chuck Berry still rocks the small basement bar here at least one Wednesday a month. The $35 tickets sell out very quickly. The venue hosts smaller-tier bands on the other nights. It has good pub food, games, darts and more.

Bridge Tap House & Wine Bar   Bar
(www.thebridgestl.com; 1004 Locust St; ⊙ 11am-1am Mon-Sat, to midnight Sun) Slip onto a sofa or rest your elbows on a table at this romantic bar where you can savor fine wines, the best local beers and a variety of exquisite little bites from a seasonal menu.

Anheuser-Busch Brewery   Brewery
(www.budweisertours.com; cnr 12th & Lynch Sts; ⊙ 10am-4pm Mon-Thu, 10am-7pm Fri & Sat, 11am-4pm Sun, from 9am Jun-Aug) FREE The world's largest beer plant gives the sort of marketing-driven tours you'd expect from the company with nearly half of the US market. View the aging cellars and famous Clydesdale horses.

☆ Entertainment

Check the Riverfront Times (www.riverfronttimes.com) for updates on entertainment options around town. Purchase tickets for most venues through MetroTix (http://metrotix.com).

Grand Center, west of downtown, is the heart of St Louis' theater scene and home of the St Louis Symphony Orchestra (www.stlsymphony.org; 718 N Grand Blvd).

The Grove, a strip of Manchester Ave between Kingshighway Blvd and S Vandeventer Ave, is the gay-and-lesbian community's hub, but Soulard, the Central West End and South Grand also have hangouts. Peruse Vital Voice (www.thevitalvoice.com) for more.

Muny   Performing Arts
(☑ 314-361-1900; www.muny.com) The Municipal Opera (aka 'Muny') hosts nightly summer musicals outdoors in Forest Park; some of the 12,000 seats are free.

Busch Stadium   Baseball
(www.stlcardinals.com; cnr Broadway & Clark Ave) The Cardinals play in this fun, retro stadium, opened in 2006. Second only to the New York Yankees in World Series wins, they last won the championship in 2011.

🔒 Shopping

The Loop and Euclid Ave in the Central West End have the best mix of local shops.

Cherokee Antique Row   Antiques
(www.cherokeeantiquerow.com; Cherokee St, east of Jefferson Ave to Indiana Ave) Six blocks of antique-filled stores in the appropriately historic Cherokee-Lemp neighborhood.

Left Bank Books   Books
(www.left-bank.com; 399 N Euclid Ave; ⊘10am-10pm Mon-Sat, 11am-6pm Sun) A great indie bookstore stocking new and used titles. There are excellent recommendations of books by local authors and frequent author readings.

❶ Information

Explore St Louis (www.explorestlouis.com; cnr 7th St & Washington Ave, America's Center; ⊘8am-5pm Mon-Sat) An excellent resource, with other branches in Kiener Plaza (corner of 6th and Chestnut) and at the airport.

Missouri Welcome Center (☑ 314-869-7100; www.visitmo.com; I-270 exit 34; ⊘8am-5pm)

KANSAS

Wicked witches and yellow-brick roads, battles over slavery and tornadoes powerful enough to pulverize entire towns are some of the more lurid images of Kansas. But the common one – amber waves of grain as far as the eye can see – is closer to reality.

There's a simple beauty to the green rolling hills and limitless horizons. Places such as Chase County beguile those who value understatement. Gems abound, from the superb space museum in Hutchinson to the indie music clubs of Lawrence. Most importantly, follow the Great Plains credo of ditching the interstate for the two-laners, and make your own discoveries. The website www.kansas-sampler.org is a brilliant resource for finding the best the state has to offer, as is the guidebook *8 Wonders of Kansas*.

❶ Information

Kansas Bed & Breakfast Association (☑ 888-572-2632; www.kbba.com)

Kansas State Parks (www.kdwpt.state.ks.us) Per vehicle per day/year $5/25. Campsites cost $7 to $13.

Kansas Travel & Tourism (☑ 785-296-2009; www.travelks.com)

OKLAHOMA

Oklahoma gets its name from the Choctaw words for 'red people.' One look at the state's vividly red earth and you'll wonder if the name is more of a sartorial than an ethnic comment. Still, with 39 tribes located here, it is a place with deep Native American significance. Museums, cultural displays and more abound.

The other side of the Old West coin, cowboys, also figure prominently in the Sooner State. Although pickups have replaced horses, there's still a great sense of the open range, interrupted only by urban Oklahoma City and Tulsa. Oklahoma's share of Route 66 links some of the Mother Road's iconic highlights and there are myriad atmospheric old towns. And just when it seems the vistas go on forever, mountains in the south and far west add texture.

❶ Information

Oklahoma Bed & Breakfast Association (☑ 866-676-5522; www.okbba.com)

Oklahoma Department of Tourism (www.travelok.com)

Oklahoma State Parks (www.travelok.com/state_parks) Most parks are free for day use; campsites cost $12 to $28 per night, and some are reservable.

Tulsa

Self-billed the 'Oil Capital of the World,' Tulsa has never dirtied its hands much with the black gold that oozes elsewhere in the state. Rather, it is home to scores of energy companies that make their living drilling for oil, selling it or supplying those who do. The steady wealth this provides once helped create Tulsa's richly detailed art-deco downtown. But today it is no longer the most charming Great Plains town: suburban sprawl has dispersed its appeal, although downtown's Brady Arts District holds promise.

👁 Sights

Downtown Tulsa has so much art-deco architecture it was once known as the 'Terra-Cotta City.' The Philcade Building (511 S Boston St), with its glorious T-shaped lobby, and Boston Avenue United Methodist Church (1301 S Boston St; ⊘8:30am-5pm Mon-Fri, 8am-5pm Sun, guided tours noon Sun), rising at the end of

National Cowboy & Western Heritage Museum, Oklahoma City

downtown, are two exceptional examples. A free walking guide from the visitor center will lead you to dozens more.

Woody Guthrie Center — Museum

(www.woodyguthriecenter.org; 102 E Brady St; adult/child $8/6; ⊙10am-6pm Tue-Sun) Woody Guthrie gained fame for his 1930s folk ballads that told stories of the Dust Bowl and the Depression. His life and music are recalled in this impressive new museum, where you can listen to his music, explore his legacy via the works of Dylan, and more.

Oklahoma Jazz Hall of Fame — Museum

(www.okjazz.org; 111 E 1st St; ⊙9am-5pm Mon & Wed-Fri, 9am-9pm Tue, noon-7pm Sun) **FREE** Tulsa's beautiful Union Station is filled with sound again, but now it is melodious rather than cacophonous. During the first half of the 20th century, Tulsa was literally at the crossroads of American music with performers both homegrown and from afar. Learn about greats like Charlie Christian, Ernie Fields Senior and Wallace Willis in detailed exhibits. Sunday jazz concerts ($15) are played at 5pm in the once-segregated grand concourse.

Gilcrease Museum — Museum

(www.gilcrease.org; 1400 Gilcrease Museum Rd; adult/child $8/free; ⊙10am-5pm Tue-Sun) Northwest of downtown, off Hwy 64, this superb American art museum sits on the manicured estate of a Native American who discovered oil on his allotment.

Philbrook Museum of Art — Museum

(www.philbrook.org; 2727 S Rockford Rd, east of Peoria Ave; adult/child $12/free; ⊙10am-5pm Tue, Wed, Fri-Sun, 10am-8pm Thu) South of town, an oil magnate's converted Italianate villa, ringed by fabulous foliage, houses some fine Native American works.

🛏 Sleeping

Chain motels aplenty line Hwy 244 and I-44, especially at the latter's exits 229 and 232. You can also recapture some of the adventure of Route 66 (but, happily, not the bugs that were once commonplace) at two restored places.

Desert Hills Motel — Motel $

(☑918-834-3311; 5220 E 11th St; r from $45; ❄ 🖥) The glowing neon cactus out front beckons you in to this lovingly restored 1950s motor court with 50 rooms (with fridges and microwaves) arranged diagonally around the parking lot. It's 5 miles east of downtown, on historic Route 66.

Hotel Campbell — Hotel $$

(☑918-744-5500; www.thecampbellhotel.com; 2636 E 11th St; r from $140; ❄ 🖥) Restored in 2011 to its 1927-era Route 66 splendor, this historic hotel east of downtown has 26 luxurious rooms with hardwood floors, and plush, period furniture. Ask for a tour.

✕ Eating & Drinking

Look for dining options in Brookside, on Peoria Ave between 31st and 51st Sts; on Historic Cherry St (now 15th St) just east of Peoria Ave; and in the Brady Arts District, centered on Brady and Main Sts immediately north of downtown.

Ike's Chili House   Diner $

(1503 E 11th St; mains under $7; ☺10am-7pm Mon-Fri, to 3pm Sat) Ike's has been serving chili for over 100 years and its classic version is much loved. You can get it straight or over Fritos, a hot dog, beans or spaghetti. Top it with red peppers, onions, jalapeños, saltines and cheddar cheese for the pure joy of it.

Elmer's   Barbecue $

(www.elmersbbqtulsa.com; 4130 S Peoria Ave; mains $7-14; ☺11am-8pm Tue-Thu, to 9pm Fri & Sat) A legendary barbecue joint where the star of the menu is the potentially deadly 'Badwich,' a bun-crushing combo of superbly smoked sausages, ham, beef, pork and more. The dining room is bright and has a house piano for the blues.

Tavern   American $$

(www.taverntulsa.com; 201 N Main St; mains $10-30; ☺11am-11pm Sun-Thu, to 1am Fri & Sat) This beautiful pub anchors the Brady Arts District and serves excellent fare. The hamburgers are legendary or you can opt for steaks, salads or seasonal specials. The bartenders are true mixologists.

☆ Entertainment

Open-air **Guthrie Green** (www.guthriegreen. com; Boston Ave & Brady St), near the namesake cultural center in the Brady Arts District, often hosts events.

Cain's Ballroom   Live Music

(www.cainsballroom.com; 423 N Main St) Rising rockers grace the boards where Bob Wills played Western swing in the '30s and the Sex Pistols caused confusion in 1978 (check out the wall Sid Vicious punched a hole in).

❶ Information

Tulsa lacks a visitor center but the Tulsa website www.visittulsa.com is useful.

Oklahoma City

Often abbreviated to OKC, Oklahoma City is nearly dead-center in the state and is the cultural and political capital. It has worked hard over the years to become more than just a cow town, all without turning its back on its cowboy heritage. It makes a good pause on your Route 66 travels.

The city is forever linked to the 1995 bombing of the Alfred P Murrah Federal Building; the memorials to this tragedy are moving and worthy stops.

◉ Sights

You'll brush up against real cowboys in **Stockyards City** (www.stockyardscity.org; Agnew Ave & Exchange Ave), southwest of downtown, either in the shops and restaurants that cater to them or at the **Oklahoma National Stockyards** (www.onsy.com; ☺auctions 8am Mon & Tue), the world's largest stocker and feeder cattle market.

Oklahoma City National
Memorial Museum   Museum

(www.oklahomacitynationalmemorial.org; 620 N Harvey Ave; adult/student $12/10; ☺9am-6pm Mon-Sat, noon-6pm Sun) The story of America's worst incident of domestic terrorism is told at this poignant museum, which avoids becoming mawkish and lets the horrible events speak for themselves. The outdoor **Symbolic Memorial** has 168 empty chair sculptures for each of the people killed in the attack (the 19 small ones are for the children who perished in the day-care center).

National Cowboy & Western
Heritage Museum   Museum

(www.nationalcowboymuseum.org; 1700 NE 63rd St; adult/child $12.50/6; ☺10am-5pm) With both art and history covered at this museum, only the smells are missing. Even if you come for just one, you're sure to be enthralled by the other. The excellent collection of Western painting and sculpture features many works by Charles M Russell and Frederic Remington.

Oklahoma History Center   Museum

(www.okhistory.org/historycenter; 800 Nazih Zuhdi Dr; adult/child $7/4; ☺10am-5pm Mon-Sat) Makes people the focus as it tells the story of the Sooner State.

🛏 Sleeping

Many older motels line I-35 south of town; newer chain properties stack up along I-44, the NW Expwy/Hwy 3 and at Bricktown (which puts you near nightlife action).

Grandison Inn at Maney Park   B&B $$

(📞405-232-8778; www.grandisoninn.com; 1200 N Shartel St; r $110-190; 🅿❄🛜) In a genteel quarter of OKC just northwest of downtown, this gracious 1904-vintage B&B welcomes guests to eight rooms with period charm and modern amenities such as DVD players. The house has amazing woodwork, including a showstopping staircase.

Colcord Hotel   Boutique Hotel $$

(📞405-601-4300; www.colcordhotel.com; 15 N Robinson Ave; r $150-200; 🅿❄@🛜) OKC's first skyscraper, built in 1910, is now a 12-story luxurious hotel. Many original flourishes, like the marble-clad lobby, survive, while the 108 rooms have a stylish, contemporary touch. It's within walking distance of Bricktown.

🍴 Eating & Drinking

Bunches of eateries cluster in Bricktown, line Western Ave between 41st and 82nd Sts, and anchor the Asian district (around 23rd St and Classen Blvd).

Tucker's Onion Burgers   Burgers $

(www.tuckersonionburgers.com; 324 NW 23rd St; mains $5.50-11; ⊙11am-9pm) 🍴 A new kind of burger joint with an old-time Route 66 vibe, Tuckers has high-quality food (locally sourced) that includes iconic OKC onion burgers, fresh-cut fries and shakes. It even has a green ethos and a fine patio.

Cattlemen's Steakhouse   Steak $$

(www.cattlemensrestaurant.com; 1309 S Agnew Ave; mains $7-25; ⊙6am-10pm Sun-Thu, to midnight Fri & Sat) OKC's most storied restaurant, this Stockyards City institution has been feeding cowpokes and city slickers slabs of beef and lamb's fries (that's a polite way of saying gonads) since 1910. Deals are still cut at the counter (where you can jump the wait for tables) and back in the luxe booths.

Ann's Chicken Fry House   Southern $$

(4106 NW 39th St; mains $4-12; ⊙11am-8:30pm Tue-Sat) Part real diner, part tourist attraction, Ann's is a Route 66 veteran renowned for its – you guessed it – chicken-fried steak. Okra and cream gravy also star, and the fried chicken lives up to the rep. Get the black-eyed peas. Cash only.

Bricktown Brewery   Brewery

(www.bricktownbrewery.com; 1 N Oklahoma Ave; ⊙11am-11pm Mon-Thu, 11am-midnight Fri & Sat, 11am-10pm Sun) A large microbrewery in Bricktown, with revelers splayed across large rooms enjoying pool, darts and just being spectators. Always hopping and has a decent food menu.

☆ Entertainment

For listings, check out the free weekly Oklahoma Gazette (www.okgazette.com) or just head to the renovated warehouses in the Bricktown District, which contain a vast array of bars, some good, some purely chain. To make a complete night of it in the district, watch the Triple A Redhawks (www.oklahomaredhawks.com; 2 Mickey Mantle Dr; tickets $5-25) play at Bricktown Ballpark. The NBA's Oklahoma City Thunder (www.nba.com/thunder; 100 W Reno Ave; tickets from $30) play nearby at Chesapeake Energy Arena.

🛍 Shopping

The Paseo Arts District isn't much more than Paseo Dr itself, but there are several art galleries and boutiques in the Spanish colonial buildings. The 16th St Plaza District is also a good bet for interesting shops.

You can buy all forms of Western wear and gear in Stockyards City, which is the real deal for cowboys and girls. Start at Langston's (www.langstons.com; 2224 Exchange Ave; ⊙10am-8pm Mon-Sat, 1-6pm Sun), which has a vast selection.

Automobile Alley, just north of downtown on N Broadway Ave, is heating up with coffee roasters, bike shops and mod mercantile stores.

ℹ Information

Oklahoma Welcome Center (📞405-478-4637; www.travelok.com; 1-35 exit 137; ⊙8am-5:30pm) Also has city info.

Bricktown, Oklahoma City

Central Route 66

From Bryce Canyon to Wheeler Peak, eye-catching natural sites abound in the Southwest. And while these landmarks are stunning, it's often the journey between them that provides the memories.

TEXAS

The Texas Panhandle isn't exactly a hub of tourism, but it does get plenty of folks passing through as they pay homage to the Mother Road. If you find yourself up thata-way, here are the top Texas stops on a Route 66 road trip, going from east to west:

Devil's Rope Museum

See p29.

Bug Ranch

(Hwy 207 access road) In response to Cadillac Ranch, five stripped-down VW bugs have sprouted 18 miles east of Amarillo.

Big Texan Steak Ranch

See p30.

Downtown Amarillo

See p30.

Cadillac Ranch

See p30.

❶ Resources:

Texas Tourism (www.traveltex.com)
TX Department of Transportation (www.txdot.gov/travel)
State Parks (tpwd.texas.gov)

NEW MEXICO

They call this the 'Land of Enchantment' for a reason. Maybe it's the drama of sunlight and shadow playing out across juniper-speckled hills; or the traditional mountain villages of horse pastures and adobe homes; or the centuries-old towns on the northern plateaus, overlooked by the magnificent Sangre de Cristos Mountains; or the volca-noes, canyons and vast desert plains spread beneath an even vaster sky. The beauty casts a powerful spell. Mud-brick churches filled with sacred art; ancient Indian pueblos; real-life cowboys and legendary outlaws; chile-smothered enchiladas – all add to the pervasive sense of otherness that of-ten makes New Mexico feel like a foreign country.

❶ Dangers & Annoyances

Albuquerque sits over 5000ft above sea level, Santa Fe and Taos are at 7000ft and the moun-tains top 13,000ft – so if you're arriving from sea level, you may feel the altitude. Take it easy for the first day or two, and be sure to drink plenty of water – a good idea, anyway, consider-ing how arid the state is. Combined with altitude, the 300-plus days of sunshine also make this an easy place to get sunburned. And New Mexico leads the nation in lightning-strike deaths per capita, so be cautious if hiking in exposed areas during monsoon thunderstorms, which can be downright apocalyptic.

If you're into outdoor adventures, your New Mexico plans may hinge on how wet or dry the year has been. Ski areas may have some of the best or worst conditions in the West depending on snowfall; national forests sometimes close completely during severe summer drought.

As Territorial Governor Lew Wallace put it back in 1880: 'Every calculation based on experience elsewhere fails in New Mexico.' Things here just don't work the way you might expect. That, paired with the *mañana* (tomorrow) mindset, may create some baffling moments. Our advice: just roll with it.

I-40 Texas to Albuquerque

As you head across the eastern half of I-40 it can be pretty tempting to keep the pedal to the metal – or set the cruise control – and power on without stopping. If you have a little time, though, some interesting historical detours beckon you off the interstate, from the days of the dinosaurs to the worst of the Wild West and some classic Route 66 kitsch.

Tucumcari

The largest I-40 town between Albuquerque and Amarillo, TX, Tucumcari is a ranching and farming community sited between the mesas and the plains that's also home to one of the best-preserved sections of Route 66. Not surprisingly, it still caters to travelers, with inexpensive motels, several classic pre-interstate buildings and souvenir shops.

◉ Sights & Activities

Drive the kids down Tucumcari's main street at night, when dozens of old neon signs cast a blazing glow. Relics of Tucumcari's Route 66 heyday, the bright, flashing signs were installed by business owners in the hope of luring tired travelers to stop for the night. Tucumcari lies barely north of I-40. Old Route 66 is the main west–east thoroughfare between exits 329 and 335, and known as Tucumcari Blvd through downtown. The principal north–south artery is 1st St.

Mesalands Dinosaur Museum   Museum
See p30.

Tucumcari Historical Museum   Museum
(☏ 575-461-4201; 416 S Adams St; adult/child $5/1; ◷ 9am-3pm Tue-Sat) Downtown museum of local history that's eclectic to say the least, with everything from a stuffed eagle and a Japanese flag to an entire firehouse and a fighter plane stranded in the yard. Several rooms feature reconstructions of early Western interiors, such as a sheriff's office, a classroom and a hospital room.

Art Murals   Walking Tour
(www.tucumcarinm.com/visitor-guide.php) Buildings on and around Route 66 in downtown Tucumcari are adorned with large murals depicting local historical highlights. The life work of artists Doug and Sharon Quarles, they can be appreciated on a mural walk that makes a great way to stretch your legs

Tucumcari Tonight mural, by artist Doug Quarles

and experience Tucumcari's Route 66 legacy. Grab a map from the website and get walking.

🛏 Sleeping

While the usual chain motels cluster around the I-40 exits, Tucumcari also boasts cool old independent motels along historic Route 66.

Blue Swallow Motel Historic Motel $

(📞 575-461-9849; www.blueswallowmotel.com; 815 E Tucumcari Blvd; r from $70; ❄ 🛜 🐾) Spend the night in this beautifully restored Route 66 motel listed on the State and National Registers of Historic Places, and feel the decades melt away. The place has a great lobby, friendly owners and vintage, uniquely decorated rooms with little chairs out on the forecourt, plus a James Dean mural, and a classic neon sign boasting '100% refrigerated air.'

Historic Route 66 Motel Motel $

(📞 575-461-1212; www.tucumcarimotel.com; 1620 E Route 66; r from $42; ❄ 🛜 🐾) When it comes to budget digs, you can't beat this historic motor-court motel, with giant plate-glass doors and mesa views; look for the light plane outside. It's nothing splashy, but the 25 rooms are cheap and clean, with comfy beds and quality pillows. Small dogs welcome, and it even has a morning-only espresso bar-cafe.

🍴 Eating & Drinking

Kix on 66 Diner $

(📞 575-461-1966; www.kixon66.com; 1102 E Tucumcari Blvd; mains $5-10; ⊙ 6am-2pm; 🛜) Popular morning hangout, within walking distance of the Blue Swallow, serving breakfast in all shapes and sizes, from *huevos rancheros* to biscuits and gravy, plus espresso coffees, doughnuts and lunch sandwiches.

Pow-Wow Restaurant & Lizard Lounge New Mexican $$

(📞 575-461-2587; www.powwowlizard.com; 801 W Tucumcari Blvd; mains $8-20; ⊙ 7am-10pm, bar until late Fri & Sat) Though it serves a reasonable food menu of steaks and Mexican specialties, the real draw here is the lounge. Thursday is karaoke night, while on most Saturdays there's live music, with big-name New Mexican bands dropping by to play a few sets.

ℹ Information

Visitor Center (📞 575-461-1694; www.tucumcarinm.com; 404 W Route 66; ⊙ 8:30am-

5pm Mon-Fri) Useful tourist information from the chamber of commerce.

ℹ Getting There & Away

Tucumcari is at the crossroads of Historic Route 66, now superceded by I-40, and US Hwy 54. It is 110 miles west of Amarillo, TX, and 170 miles east of Albuquerque.

Santa Rosa

Settled by Hispanic farmers in the mid-19th century, Santa Rosa's modern claim to fame is, weirdly enough, as the scuba diving capital of the Southwest. There's not much else going on here, though.

👁 Sights & Activities

Take exit 273 from Route 66/I-40 to reach downtown. Having started as Coronado St, the main street becomes Parker Ave through downtown, and then Will Rogers Dr when it passes exits 275 and 277.

Blue Hole Lake

(📞 575-472-3763; www.santarosanm.org; Hwy 40/US 66) One of the 10 best dive spots in the US is, surprisingly, right here in li'l ol' Santa Rosa. The bell-shaped, 81ft-deep Blue Hole, downtown, is 80ft in diameter at the surface and widens to 130ft down below. Fed by a natural spring flowing at 3000 gallons a minute, the water is both very clear and pretty cool (at around 67°F/17°C). Platforms for divers are suspended about 25ft down. There's a dive shop onsite.

Route 66 Auto Museum Museum

(www.route66automuseum.com; 2766 Rte 66; admission $5; ⊙ 7:30am-6pm Mon-Sat, 10am-5pm Sun Apr-Oct, 8am-5pm Mon-Sat, 10am-5pm Sun Nov-Mar) This museum pays homage to the mother of all roads. Boasting around 35 cars from the 1920s through the 1960s, all in beautiful condition, plus lots of 1950s memorabilia, it's a fun place; enjoy a milkshake at the '50s-style snack shack. If you're in the market for a beautifully restored old Chevy, friendly owner 'Bozo' also deals in antique cars.

Puerto de Luna Historic Site

The tiny village of Puerto de Luna, beside the Pecos River 10 miles south of Santa Rosa, was founded in the 1860s. The drive there is pretty, winding through arroyos surrounded by eroded sandstone mesas on Hwy 91. Once you arrive you'll find an old county courthouse, a village church and a bunch of weathered adobe buildings. It's all quite charming, so long as you're not in a hurry to do something else.

🎪 Festivals & Events

Route 66 Festival   Car Show

(⊘ Aug/Sep) In keeping with the Route 66 theme, this auto-centric show, held in August or September, attracts vintage- and classic-car enthusiasts, as well as folks driving strange things on wheels.

🛏 Sleeping & Eating

Main street Santa Rosa holds plenty of family-owned diners and roadside cafes, abounding in Route 66 allure. Chain hotels cluster around the I-40 exits.

Joseph's Route 66 Diner   Diner $$

(☑ 575-472-3361; 1775 Historic Route 66; mains $7-21; ⊘ 8am-10pm) Route 66 nostalgia lines the walls of this popular place, family-run since 1956. The bountiful Mexican and American menu ranges from Santa Fe enchiladas with blue corn tortillas to catfish, burgers and steaks. Joseph's also mixes some serious margaritas.

Silver Moon   Diner $$

(☑ 505-472-3162; 2545 Historic Route 66; mains $9-17; ⊘ 6am-10pm) This trademark Route 66 eatery first opened its doors in 1959, and serves fantastic homemade *chile rellenos* (stuffed chile peppers) and other tasty diner grub dressed up with a New Mexican twist. It's popular with travelers following Route 66's old roadhouse trail, as well as locals who come for a morning coffee and a plate of bacon and eggs.

Albuquerque

This bustling desert crossroads has an understated charm, one based more on its locals than on any kind of urban sparkle. In New Mexico's largest city, immediately west of the Sandia mountains at the point where the east–west Route 66 bridges the north–south Rio Grande, folks are more than happy to share history, highlights and must-try restaurants.

Centuries-old adobes pepper the lively Old Town area, and the shops, restaurants and bars in the hip Nob Hill zone are all within easy walking distance. Good hiking trails abound just outside of town, through evergreen forests or among panels of ancient petroglyphs, while the city's modern museums explore space and nuclear energy. There's a vibrant mix of university students, Native Americans, Hispanics and gays and lesbians. You'll find fliers for square dances and yoga classes distributed with equal enthusiasm, and see ranch hands and real-estate brokers chowing down beside each other at hole-in-the-wall *taquerías* (Mexican fast-food restaurants) and retro cafes.

- -

👁 Sights

Central Ave, the former Route 66, is still Albuquerque's main street, passing from

ALBUQUERQUE IN...

One Day

Jump-start your belly with a plate of *huevos rancheros* (fried eggs in a spicy tomato sauce, served atop tortillas) from Frontier (p77), before heading to the Indian Pueblo Cultural Center (p75), for a heads-up introduction to Pueblo traditions and culture.

Next up visit the BioPark (p75), which has a zoo, aquarium, botanical gardens and nature trails along the bosk. Head back into town for a bite at Golden Crown Panaderia (p77), then wander over to Old Town (p73) for the afternoon. Walk off lunch admiring the San Felipe de Neri Church (p75), browsing the galleries around the plaza and catching up on your snake trivia at the American International Rattlesnake Museum (p75). Dine outdoors in Nob Hill (p77); Albuquerque's grooviest neighborhood is thick with restaurants.

Two Days

Wander around the Petroglyph National Monument (p75), then head over to Loyola's for lunch before blowing your mind at the National Museum of Nuclear Science & History. Reach the top of Sandia Crest before sunset, either by Tramway or by scenic road, for expansive views of the Rio Grande Valley. When you come back down, linger over delicious food and wine at the Slate Street Cafe & Wine Loft (p77).

Albuquerque

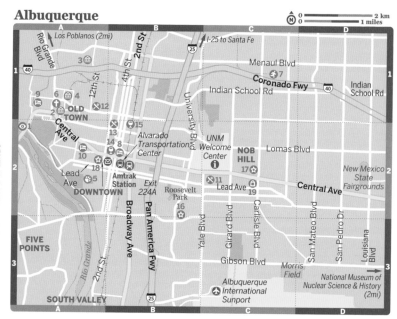

Albuquerque

◉ Sights
1 Albuquerque Aquarium A2
2 American International Rattlesnake ....
   Museum.............................. A1
   Botanic Garden .... see 1
3 Indian Pueblo Cultural Center A1
4 New Mexico Museum of Natural
   History & Science A1
5 Rio Grande Zoo A2
6 San Felipe de Neri Church.............. A1

➕ Activities
7 Stone Age Climbing Gym.............. C1

🛏 Sleeping
8 Andaluz B2
9 Econo Lodge Old Town................ A1
10 Route 66 Hostel...................... A2

✖ Eating
11 Frontier C2
12 Golden Crown Panaderia.............. A1
13 Slate Street Cafe & Wine Loft........... B2

☕ Drinking & Nightlife
14 Anodyne............................. B2
15 Marble Brewery B2
   Satellite Coffee..................... see 11

★ Entertainment
16 Albuquerque Isotopes B2
17 Guild Cinema C2
   KiMo Theatre .... see 14
18 Launch Pad.......................... A2
   Popejoy Hall .... see 11

🛍 Shopping
19 Mariposa Gallery C2

east to west through the state fairground, Nob Hill, the University of New Mexico (UNM), downtown and Old Town before crossing the Rio Grande. Street addresses often conclude with a directional designation, such as Wyoming NE, that specifies one of the city's four quadrants: the center

point is where Central Ave crosses the railroad tracks, just to the east of the downtown area.

Albuquerque's top sights are primarily concentrated in and around the Old Town and beside the river, but several interesting attractions – including the Indian Pueblo

Cultural Center, Petroglyph National Monument and Sandia Peak Tramway – lie further afield, and are only readily accessible by car.

New Mexico Museum of
Natural History & Science   Museum
(www.nmnaturalhistory.org; 1801 Mountain Rd NW; adult/child $7/4; ⊙9am-5pm; 👶) Dinosaur-mad kids are certain to love this huge modern museum, on the northeastern fringes of Old Town. From the T Rex in the main atrium onwards, it's crammed with ferocious ancient beasts. The emphasis throughout is on New Mexico, with dramatic displays on the state's geological origins, details of the impact of climate change, and also an exhibit on Albuquerque's role in computer history – did you know this is where Microsoft first started out?

American International
Rattlesnake Museum   Museum
(www.rattlesnakes.com; 202 San Felipe St NW; adult/child $5/3; ⊙10am-6pm Mon-Sat, 1-5pm Sun Jun-Aug, 11:30am-5:30pm Mon-Fri, 10am-6pm Sat, 1-5pm Sun Sep-May) Anyone charmed by snakes and all things slithery will find this museum fascinating; for ophidiaphobes, it's a complete nightmare, filled with the world's largest collection of different rattlesnake species. You'll also find snake-themed beer bottles and postmarks from every town named 'Rattlesnake' in the US.

San Felipe de Neri Church   Church
(www.sanfelipedeneri.org; Old Town Plaza; ⊙7am-5:30pm daily, museum 9:30am-5pm Mon-Sat) Dating in its present incarnation from 1793, the facade of this adobe church now provides Old Town's most famous photo op. Mass is celebrated Monday, Tuesday, Wednesday and Friday at 7am, with Sunday Mass at 7am, 10:15am and noon.

Albuquerque BioPark   Park
Especially for anyone traveling with kids, the riverside Albuquerque BioPark makes a wonderful escape from the city's summer heat. A combo ticket, sold until noon daily, covers its three main attractions: an aquarium (✆505-764-6200; www.cabq.gov/biopark; 2601 Central Ave NW; adult/child $12.50/4, combo ticket for 3 sites $20/6; ⊙9am-5pm, to 6pm Sat & Sun Jun-Aug; 📷) and botanic garden (www.cabq.gov/biopark; 2601 Central Ave NW; adult/child $12.50/4, combo ticket for 3 sites $20/6; ⊙9am-5pm, until 6pm Sat & Sun Jun-Aug) just west of Old Town, and a zoo (✆505-768-2000; www.cabq.gov/bio

park; 903 10th St SW; adult/child $12.50/4, combo ticket for 3 sites $20/6; ⊙9am-5pm, to 6pm Sat & Sun Jun-Aug) further south. The park also includes the open space of Tingley Beach – in truth, more of a fishing lake than a beach – to which access is free.

Indian Pueblo
Cultural Center   Museum
(IPCC; ✆505-843-7270; www.indianpueblo.org; 2401 12th St NW; adult/child $6/3; ⊙9am-5pm) Collectively run by New Mexico's 19 Pueblos, this cultural center makes an essential stop-off during even the shortest Albuquerque visit. The museum downstairs holds fascinating displays on the Pueblos' collective history and individual artistic traditions, while the galleries above offer changing temporary exhibitions. They're arrayed in a crescent around a plaza that's regularly used for dances and crafts demonstrations, and as well as the recommended Pueblo Harvest Cafe there's also a large gift shop and retail gallery.

Petroglyph National
Monument   Archaeological Site
(✆505-899-0205; www.nps.gov/petr; 6001 Unser Blvd NW; ⊙visitor center 8am-5pm) 🅿 The lava field preserved in this large desert park, west of the Rio Grande, is adorned with more than 20,000 ancient petroglyphs. Take exit 154 off I-40 to reach the visitor center, 5.5 miles northwest of Old Town, and choose a hiking trail. Boca Negra Canyon is the busiest; Rinconada Canyon – the longest at 2.2 miles round-trip – offers the most solitude; and Piedras Marcadas holds 300 petroglyphs. Smash-and-grab thefts have been reported, so don't leave valuables in your vehicle.

🏃 Activities
The ideal way to get out into the fresh air in Albuquerque, and explore the city under your own steam, is to traverse the city by bike. Cycling is a big deal here, for commuting locals and national-level competitors alike. For details of the excellent network of cycling lanes, which include the stretch of Central Ave between Old Town and downtown as well as dedicated off-road tracks along arroyos, download the city map at www.cabq.gov/bike.

Elena Gallegos Open Space   Hiking
(www.cabq.gov; Simms Park Rd; weekday/weekend parking $1/2; ⊙7am-9pm Apr-Oct, closes 7pm Nov-Mar) Sandia Crest is Albuquerque's

outdoor playground, popular for skiing and hiking. As well as several picnic areas, this foothills park holds trailheads for hiking, running and mountain-biking; some routes are wheelchair-accessible. Come early before the sun gets too hot or late, to enjoy the panoramic views at sunset, as the city lights start to twinkle below. Time evening walks carefully, though; darkness falls quickly and howling coyotes ring the park. They won't bother you, but it can be unnerving.

Routes Rentals Cycling

(☑505-933-5667; www.routesrentals.com; 404 San Felipe St NW; tours incl rental from $30;

⊙8am-7pm Mon-Fri, 7am-7pm Sat & Sun) This friendly Old Town cycle shop rents out all kinds of bikes from $20 for a half-day, and also runs a great program of guided cycling tours, including a daily riverside trip and several routes focused on hit TV series *Breaking Bad*.

Stone Age Climbing Gym Rock climbing

(☑505-341-2016; www.climbstoneage.com; 4130 Cutler Ave NE; day pass $16; ⊙noon-11pm Mon-Fri, 10am-9pm Sat & Sun) While there are lots of great climbing routes in the Sandias, rock climbers itching to hit the wall will also dig this gym, offering 21,000 sq ft of climbing terrain simulating a wide range of rock features.

ALBUQUERQUE'S MOUNTAIN: SANDIA CREST

Albuquerqueans always know which way is east thanks to 10,378ft Sandia Crest, sacred to Sandia Pueblo and well named for both its wavelike silhouette and the glorious pink (*sandia* is Spanish for 'watermelon') its granite cliffs glow at sunset. There are three ways to the top.

» Beautiful 8-mile (one-way) La Luz Trail (FR 444; parking $3) is the most rewarding, rising 3800ft from the desert, past a small waterfall to pine forests and spectacular views. It gets hot, so start early. Take Tramway Blvd east from I-25, then turn left on FR 333 to the trailhead.

» Sandia Peak Tramway (☑505-856-7325; www.sandiapeak.com; 30 Tramway Rd NE; parking $1, adult/youth 13-20yr/child $20/17/12; ⊙9am-0pm Jun-Aug, 9am-8pm Wed-Mon, from 5pm Tue Sep-May) is the most extravagant route to the summit; ride round-trip or take the tram up and then hike down La Luz, walking 2 miles more on Tramway Trail to your car.

» Finally you can drive, via Hwy 14, making a left onto Sandia Crest Rd (Hwy 165). The road is lined with trailheads and picnic spots (a daily $3 parking fee covers all of them), and low-impact camping ($3) is allowed by permit throughout Cibola National Forest. The choices are endless, but don't skip the easy mile round-trip to Sandia Man Cave, where one of the earliest known human encampments in North America was discovered in 1936; bring a flashlight. The trailhead is along Hwy 165, north of the spur road to Sandia Crest.

At the top, the Sandia Crest Visitor Center (☑505-248-0190; Hwy 165; ⊙10am-sunset in winter, to 7pm in summer) offers nature programs daily; Sandia Crest House (☑505-243-0605; www.sandiacresthouse.com; dishes $4-9; ⊙10am-5pm), in the same building, serves burgers and snacks. This is the jumping-off point for the exquisite Sandia Crest Trail. With incredible views either way you go, paths lead north along the ridgeline for 11 miles and south along the ridge for 16 miles.

Take the trail 2 miles south, past Kiwanis Cabin rock house, to the tram terminal and High Finance (☑505-243-9742; www.sandiapeakrestaurants.com; lunch mains $7-15, dinner mains $20-38; ⊙11am-3pm Wed-Sun, 4:30-9pm daily), where the food is nothing special but the views are fabulous.

This is also the site of Sandia Peak Ski Park (☑505-242-9052; www.sandiapeak.com; lift tickets adult/child $50/40; ⊙9am-4pm Dec-Mar & Jun-Sep), a smallish but scenic ski area. In summer, the park has a bike-and-lift combo for $58 (with $650 deposit) – you get a bike and lift pass to blaze those downhill runs all day long (note that bikes aren't allowed on the tram).

Classes are offered and you can rent gear. To get here, take the Carlisle exit off I-40.

🛏 Sleeping

Although Albuquerque holds about 150 hotels – all of which fill during the International Balloon Fiesta and the Gathering of Nations – few are in any way exceptional. If you're looking for character or charm, a B&B makes a better option.

The cheapest motels of all line Central Ave, especially around the I-25 on-ramp and east of Nob Hill. You can usually score a room for under $50, but some can be pretty sleazy. Smarter chain hotels gather a little further south, close to the airport and UNM.

Econo Lodge Old Town   Motel $

(☑505-243-8475; www.econolodge.com; 2321 Central Ave NW; r incl breakfast $69; P✳@🅿🛍) Just five minutes' walk west of the plaza, this bright, clean motel makes a great deal for anyone planning to explore the Old Town or the BioPark, with spacious and well-equipped modern rooms, an indoor pool and free hot breakfasts.

Route 66 Hostel   Hostel $

(☑505-247-1813; www.rt66hostel.com; 1012 Central Ave SW; dm $20, r from $25; P@🅿) This pastel-lemon hostel, in a former residence a few blocks west of downtown, holds male and female dorms plus simple private rooms, some of which share bathrooms. The beds are aging, but there's a welcoming atmosphere, with common facilities including a library and a kitchen offering free self-serve breakfasts. Voluntary chores; no check-ins between 1:30pm and 4:30pm.

Andaluz   Boutique Hotel $$

(☑505-242-9090; www.hotelandaluz.com; 125 2nd St NW; r $112-279; P✳@🅿) Albuquerque's finest historic hotel, built in the heart of downtown in 1939, has been modernized while retaining period details like its stunning central atrium, where cozy arched nooks hold tables and couches. Rooms feature hypoallergenic bedding and carpets, the Más Tapas Y Vino restaurant is excellent, and there's a rooftop bar. Reserve 30 days in advance for the best rates.

Los Poblanos   B&B $$$

(☑505-344-9297; www.lospoblanos.com; 4803 Rio Grande Blvd NW; r $180-330; P✳@🅿) This amazing 20-room B&B, on a 1930s rural ranch that's a National Historic Place, is five minutes' drive north of Old Town. Close to the Rio Grande, it's set amid 25 acres of gardens, lavender fields (blooming mid-June through July) and an organic farm. The gorgeous rooms feature kiva fireplaces, while produce from the farm is served for breakfast.

🍴 Eating

Albuquerque offers plenty of definitive down-home New Mexican grub, plus the region's widest variety of international cuisines. It's not a foodie destination like Santa Fe, and restaurants geared towards tourists tend to be less than outstanding. To browse options from hip to homey, budget to blow-out, the Nob Hill district, around the University, is by far the best bet.

Golden Crown Panaderia   Bakery $

(☑505-243-2424; www.goldencrown.biz; 1103 Mountain Rd NW; mains $7-20; ⊙7am-8pm Tue-Sat, 10am-8pm Sun) Who doesn't love a friendly neighborhood cafe-bakery? Especially one in a cozy old adobe, with gracious staff, oven-fresh bread and pizza, fruity empanadas, smooth espresso coffees and free cookies all round? Call ahead to reserve a loaf of quick-selling green chile bread – then eat it hot, out on the patio.

Frontier   New Mexican $

(☑505-266-0550; www.frontierrestaurant.com; 2400 Central Ave SE; mains $3-12; ⊙5am-1am; 🅿♿) Get in line for enormous cinnamon rolls (made with lots of butter) and some of the best *huevos rancheros* (fried eggs in a spicy tomato sauce, served atop tortillas) in town. The food, people-watching and Western art are all outstanding.

Slate Street Cafe & Wine Loft   Modern American $$

(☑505-243-2210; www.slatestreetcafe.com; 515 Slate St; breakfast $6-12, lunch $9-16, dinner $12-28; ⊙7:30am-3pm Mon-Fri, 9am-2pm Sat & Sun, 5-9pm Tue-Thu, 5-10pm Fri & Sat) Popular downtown rendezvous, off 6th St NW, just north of Lomas Blvd. The cafe downstairs is usually packed with people enjoying imaginative Southwestern/American comfort food, from peanut butter and jelly sandwiches to herb-crusted pork chops, while the upstairs wine loft serves 25 wines by the glass and offers regular tasting sessions.

🍷 Drinking

Albuquerque's bar scene, which has long focused on downtown and Nob Hill, has been enlivened in recent years by the emergence of a new breed of brewpubs scattered across the city.

Satellite Coffee
Cafe

(www.satellitecoffee.com; 2300 Central Ave SE; ⊙ 6am-11pm Mon-Fri, from 7am Sat & Sun; 🛜) Albuquerque's answer to Starbucks lies in these hip coffee shops – look for the other eight locations around town – luring lots of laptop-toting regulars. Set up and still owned by the same brilliant folks responsible for the Flying Star chain.

Anodyne
Bar

(☑ 505-244-1820; www.theanodyne.com; 409 Central Ave NW; ⊙ 4pm-1:30am Mon-Sat, 7-11:30pm Sun) An excellent spot for a game of pool, Anodyne is a huge space with book-lined walls, wood ceilings, plenty of overstuffed chairs, more than 100 bottled beers and great people-watching on Central Ave.

Marble Brewery
Brewery

(☑ 505-243-2739; www.marblebrewery.com; 111 Marble Ave NW; ⊙ noon-midnight, to 10:30pm Sun) Popular downtown brewpub, attached to its namesake brewery, with a snug interior for winter nights and a beer garden where local bands play early-evening gigs in summer. Be sure to try their 11%-strength Imperial Stout.

☆ Entertainment

For comprehensive listings of Albuquerque's many nightspots and a calendar of upcoming events, pick up the free weekly *Alibi* (www.alibi.com), published every Tuesday. Friday's *Albuquerque Journal* is helpful, too. Downtown has a great nightlife scene, while the proximity of UNM makes Nob Hill pretty lively too. The UNM Lobos (www.golobos.com) has a full roster of sports teams, but is best known for basketball (men's and women's) and women's volleyball.

Launch Pad
Live Music

(☑ 505-764-8887; www.launchpadrocks.com; 618 Central Ave SW) This retro-modern place is the hottest stage for local live music.

Guild Cinema
Cinema

(☑ 505-255-1848; www.guildcinema.com; 3405 Central Ave NE; admission $8) The only independently owned, single-screen theater in town programs great indie, avant-garde, Hollywood fringe, political and international features. Stick around for discussions following select films.

Albuquerque Isotopes
Baseball

(www.albuquerquebaseball.com; Ave Cesar Chavez, Isotopes Park, University SE) First of all: yes, the city's baseball team really was named for the episode of *The Simpsons*, 'Hungry, Hungry Homer,' when America's favorite TV dad tried to keep his beloved Springfield Isotopes from moving to Albuquerque. The 'topes sell more merchandise than any other minor (and most major) league team. They sometimes win, too.

🛍 Shopping

Albuquerque's most interesting shops are in Old Town and Nob Hill.

Mariposa Gallery
Arts & Crafts

(☑ 505-268-6828; www.mariposa-gallery.com; 3500 Central Ave SE) Beautiful, funky arts, crafts and jewelry, by regional artists.

Silver Sun
Jewelry

(☑ 505-246-9692; www.silversunalbuquerque.com; 116 San Felipe St NW; ⊙ 9am-4pm) A reputable Old Town store specializing in natural

---

PERFORMING ARTS

Downtown's historic KiMo Theatre and Popejoy Hall (www.popejoypresents.com; Central Ave, at Cornell St SE) on the UNM campus are the premier venues for music and contemporary drama, with both the New Mexico Ballet Company (www.newmexicoballet.org; tickets $11-24) and the New Mexico Philharmonic (www.nmphil.org) performing busy seasons at Popejoy Hall and other venues. These days, the biggest pop, rock and country stars are being lured away from the city proper to play the nearby casinos, especially Sandia Casino.

American turquoise, as stones as well as finished jewelry.

❶ Information

INTERNET RESOURCES

Albuquerque Online (www.abqonline.com) Exhaustive listings and links for local businesses.

City of Albuquerque (www.cabq.gov) Public transportation, area attractions and more.

TOURIST INFORMATION

Albuquerque Convention & Visitors Bureau (☑ 505-842-9918; www.itsatrip.org; 20 First Plaza NW, cnr 2nd St & Copper Ave; ⊙ 9am-4pm Mon-Fri)

Old Town Information Center (☑ 505-243-3215; www.itsatrip.org; 303 Romero Ave NW; ⊙ 10am-5pm Oct-May, to 6pm Jun-Sep)

❶ Getting Around

Albuquerque is an easy city to drive around. Streets are wide and there's usually metered or even free parking within blocks from wherever you want to stop.

Santa Fe architecture
P_WEI / GETTY IMAGES ©

Santa Fe

Welcome to 'the city different,' a place that makes its own rules without ever forgetting its long and storied past. Walking through its historic neighborhoods, or around the busy Plaza that remains its core, there's no denying that Santa Fe has a timeless, earthy soul. Founded around 1610, Santa Fe is the second-oldest city and the oldest state capital in the US, and is all but unique in having not only preserved many of its seductive original adobe buildings, but also insisted that all new downtown structures follow the same architectural style. And yet, despite being home to the country's oldest public building and throwing its oldest annual party, Fiesta, Santa Fe is also synonymous with contemporary chic, thanks to its thriving art market, gourmet restaurants, great museums, upscale spas and world-class opera.

At over 7000ft above sea level, Santa Fe is also the nation's highest state capital. Sitting at the foot of the glowing Sangre de Cristo range, it makes a fantastic base for hiking, mountain-biking, backpacking and skiing. When you come off the trails, you can indulge in chile-smothered local cuisine, buy turquoise and silver directly from Native American jewelers in the Plaza, visit remarkable churches, or simply wander along centuries-old, cottonwood-shaded lanes and daydream about some day moving here.

◉ Sights

For a city of its size, Santa Fe punches way above its weight. Not only is its small downtown core still filled with Colonial-era adobe homes and churches, with the region's Native American heritage everywhere apparent, but they've been joined by an array of world-class museums and art galleries. There's also a separate cluster of wonderful museums on Museum Hill, a short drive southeast.

◉ Downtown

Downtown Santa Fe still centers on its historic Plaza and the grid of streets that surrounds it. It's easy to while away a full day within these few blocks, punctuating visits to the art and history museums with downtime in the countless cafes, restaurants and shops.

Across the Santa Fe River – dry for much of the year, but lined by verdant footpaths – lie the official buildings of New Mexico's state government. The Guadalupe and Railyard districts, home to lively bars and restaurants, are immediately west, while gallery-lined Canyon Rd stretches away east.

SANTA FE IN...

Two Days

After breakfast at Cafe Pasqual's, art up at the Georgia O'Keeffe Museum. Stroll around the Plaza, checking out the Native American jewelry being sold on the sidewalk, then pop into the historic Palace of the Governors. Have a classic (and cheap) New Mexican lunch at Tia Sophia's before heading over to check out the galleries along Canyon Rd. For dinner, hit the Tune-Up Cafe for casual local dining.

The next morning, chow down at the Santa Fe Baking Co. Head over to Museum Hill, prioritizing the fabulous Museum of International Folk Art. Pop into Harry's Roadhouse for lunch, then take a scenic drive up Ski Basin Rd, where there are loads of hiking and biking trails. Have dinner and catch some live music at the city's oldest tavern, El Farol. Olé!

Three Days

After two days in town, grab breakfast at the Tesuque Village Market, then head on up to Bandelier National Monument to hike through the canyon and climb ladders to reach ancient cliffside kivas. Then it's back to Santa Fe for a dinner of barbecue brisket quesadillas and a Mescal margarita or two at the Cowgirl Hall of Fame.

The Plaza
Plaza

For over 400 years, the Plaza has stood at the heart of Santa Fe. Originally it marked the far northern end of the Camino Real from Mexico; later, it was the goal for wagons heading west along the Santa Fe Trail. Today, this grassy square is peopled by tourists, wandering from museum to margarita; food vendors; skateboarding kids; and street musicians. Beneath the portico of the Palace of the Governors, along its northern side, Pueblo Indians sell jewelry and pottery.

Palace of the Governors
Historic Building

(☑505-476-5100; www.palaceofthegovernors.org; 105 W Palace Ave; adult/child $9/free; ⏰10am-5pm, closed Mon Oct-May) The oldest public building in the US, this low-slung adobe complex started out as home to New Mexico's first Spanish governor in 1610; was occupied by Pueblo Indians following their Revolt in 1680; and after 1846 became the seat of the US Territory's earliest governors. It now holds fascinating displays on Santa Fe's multi-faceted past, and some superb Hispanic religious artworks, while its modern adjunct alongside, the New Mexico History Museum, tells the story of the state as a whole.

Georgia O'Keeffe Museum
Museum

(☑505-946-1000; www.okeeffemuseum.org; 217 Johnson St; adult/child $12/free; ⏰10am-5pm, to 7pm Fri) With 10 beautifully lit galleries in a rambling 20th-century adobe, this museum boasts the world's largest collection of O'Keeffe's work. She's best known for her luminous New Mexican landscapes, but the changing exhibitions here range through her entire career, focusing, for example, on her years in New York. Major museums worldwide own her most famous canvases, so you may not see familiar paintings, but you're sure to be bowled over by the thick brushwork and transcendent colors on show.

Visit the museum website to reserve a tour of O'Keeffe's former home, in the village of Abiquiú, 50 miles northwest of Santa Fe.

◉ Museum Hill

Four of Santa Fe's finest museums stand together on Museum Hill, 2 miles southwest of the Plaza. This low but beautifully situated mountain-view hillock is not a neighborhood in any sense – all the museums hold superb gift shops, but there's nothing else here, apart from a research library and a recommended cafe. Neither is it a good walking destination; if you can't drive or cycle, use the Santa Fe Trails bus network, catching either the M Line, or, between May and mid-October, the free Pick-Up.

Museum of International Folk Art
Museum

(☑505-827-6344; www.internationalfolkart.org; 706 Camino Lejo; adult/child $9/free; ⏰10am-5pm, closed Mon Sep-May) Santa Fe's most unusual and exhilarating museum centers on the world's largest collection of folk art.

Its huge main gallery displays whimsical and mind-blowing objects from more than 100 different countries. Tiny human figures go about their business in fully realized village and city scenes, while dolls, masks, toys and garments spill across the walls. Changing exhibitions in other wings explore vernacular art and culture worldwide. Try to hit the incredible International Folk Art Market, held here in mid-July.

Museum of Indian Arts & Culture
Museum

(www.indianartsandculture.org; 710 Camino Lejo; adult/child $9/free; ⊙ 10am-5pm, closed Mon Sep-May) This top-quality museum sets out to trace the origins and history of the various Native American peoples of the entire desert Southwest, and explain and illuminate their widely differing cultural traditions. Pueblo, Navajo and Apache interviewees describe the contemporary realities each group now faces, while a truly superb collection of ceramics, modern and ancient, is complemented by stimulating temporary displays.

🏃 Activities

Santa Fe's cultural attractions may be second to none, but visitors do not live by art appreciation alone. Get thee to the great outdoors. The best one-stop spot to peruse your options is the Public Lands Information Center (p88), inconveniently located south of town off of Hwy 14.

Before heading out for any strenuous activities, remember the elevations here abouts; take time to acclimatize, and watch for signs of altitude sickness if you're going high. Weather changes rapidly in the mountains, and summer storms are frequent, especially in the afternoons, so keep an eye on the sky and hike prepared. Most trails are usually closed by snow in winter, and higher trails may be closed through May.

TOP FIVE SANTA FE DAY HIKES

There are a ton of trails around Santa Fe. Whether you're looking for all-day adventure or a relaxing stroll through a special landscape, you'll find it. Trailheads for all the hikes below are within an hour's drive from the Plaza.

Raven's Ridge Starting along the Upper Winsor Trail from the ski basin parking lot, Raven's Ridge cuts east after the first steep mile of switchbacks to follow the Pecos Wilderness boundary high above the treeline to the top of Lake Peak (12,409ft). A strenuous hike at substantial elevation, it's well worth it if your body can take it. No trail has better views; you can see forever from up here. Loop back by hiking down the ski slopes to complete a round-trip of about 4 miles.

Upper Winsor After its steep first mile from the ski basin, the Upper Winsor Trail mellows out, contouring around forested slopes with a moderate uphill section toward the end. Puerto Nambé (11,050ft), a huge and beautiful meadow in the saddle between Santa Fe Baldy (12,622ft) to the north and Penitente Peak (12,249ft) to the south, is a great place for a picnic. The round-trip is about 10 miles.

Aspen Vista The premier path for immersing yourself in the magical fall foliage, this trail lives up to its name. The first mile or so is supereasy, gaining little elevation and following an old dirt road. It gets a little more difficult the further you go; just turn back when you've had enough. The trailhead is at about 10,000ft, along the road to the ski basin; it's marked 'Trail No 150.' Mountain bikers love this one, too.

La Cieneguilla Petroglyph Site Half a mile along a dirt track from a clearly marked trailhead on Airport Rd, 12 miles southwest of downtown, this trail climbs the low hillside to reach a rocky bluff that's covered with ancient Keresan petroglyphs, including images of the flute player Kokopelli. Allow an hour's hiking time in total.

Tent Rocks There's truly surreal hiking at Kasha-Katuwe Tent Rocks National Monument, near Cochiti Pueblo 40 miles southwest of Santa Fe, where short trails meander through a geologic wonderland.

Downtown Santa Fe

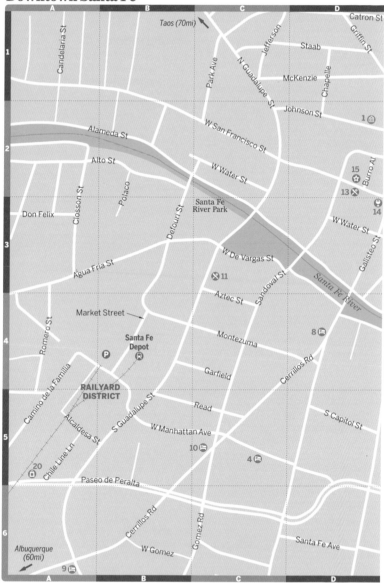

Catron St
Taos (70mi)
Candelaria St
Park Ave
N Guadalupe St
Jefferson
Staab
Griffin St
McKenzie
Chapelle
Johnson St
1
W San Francisco St
Alameda St
Alto St
W Water St
Burro Al
15
Polaco
Closson St
Detouri St
Santa Fe
River Park
13
14
Don Felix
W Water St
W De Vargas St
Galisteo St
Agua Fria St
Santa Fe River
11
Sandoval St
Aztec St
Market Street
Montezuma
8
Romero St
Santa Fe
Depot
Cerrillos Rd
Garfield
Camino de la Familia
RAILYARD
DISTRICT
S Capitol St
Read
Alcaldesa St
S Guadalupe St
W Manhattan Ave
Chile Line Ln
10
4
20
Paseo de Peralta
Cerrillos Rd
Gomez Rd
Santa Fe Ave
Albuquerque
(60mi)
W Gomez
9

The best local map for hiking trails and
outdoor action is the *Santa Fe/Bandelier/
Los Alamos* map, which is published by Sky
Terrain.

🛏 Sleeping

When it comes to luxury accommodations,
Santa Fe boasts more than its share of opu-
lent hotels and posh B&Bs, with some un-
forgettable historic options within a block
of the Plaza. Rates steadily diminish the

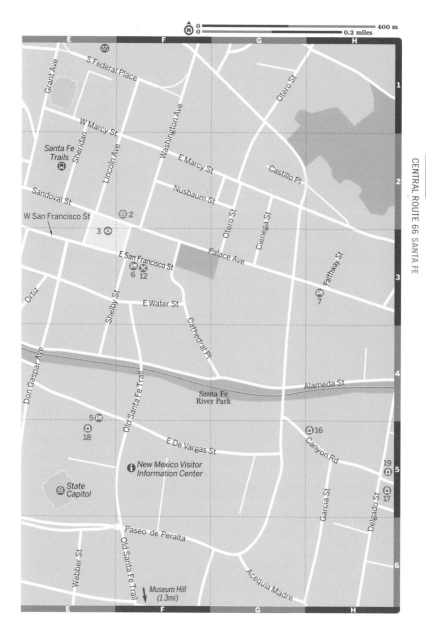

further you go from downtown, with low-budget and national chain options strung out along Cerrillos Rd toward I-25.

Santa Fe has two peak seasons, when you should book well in advance and can expect to pay premium prices: summer, particularly during Indian Market in August and on opera nights, and also December. January and February are the cheapest months. Room rates shown here do not include taxes and other add-ons, which can total 11% to 15%.

Downtown Santa Fe

◎ Sights
1 Georgia O'Keeffe Museum..........D2
2 Palace of the Governors............F2
3 The Plaza......................E3

⊕ Activities
La Posada Spa ....see 7

⊜ Sleeping
4 El Paradero.......................C5
5 Inn of the Five Graces...............E4
6 La Fonda F3
7 La Posada de Santa Fe..............H3
8 Old Santa Fe Inn.....................D4
9 Sage Inn............................A6
10 Santa Fe Motel & Inn...............C5

✖ Eating
11 Cowgirl Hall of Fame................C3
   French Pastry Shop ....see 6
12 La Plazuela F3
13 Tia Sophia's.......................D3

◎ Drinking & Nightlife
Bell Tower Bar ....see 6
14 Evangelo's.........................D3

✿ Entertainment
15 Lensic Performing Arts Center D2

⊜ Shopping
16 Adobe Gallery......................H5
17 Economos/Hampton Galleries H5
18 GF Contemporary E5
19 LoneDog NoiseCat H5
20 Santa Fe Farmers Market A5

Santa Fe National Forest and Hyde State Park are the best nearby locations for car camping. Stop by the Public Lands Information Center for information.

Silver Saddle Motel   Motel $

(☎505-471-7663;   www.santafesilversaddlemotel. com; 2810 Cerrillos Rd; r from $62; P✳@⊛⊛) This old-fashioned, even kitschy Route 66 motel compound, 3 miles southwest of the Plaza, offers the best budget value in town. Some rooms have pleasant tiled kitchenettes, while all have shady wooden arcades outside and comfortable cowboy-inspired decor inside – get the Kenny Rogers or Wyatt Earp rooms if you can. Rates include continental breakfast.

Santa Fe International Hostel   Hostel $

(☎505-988-1153;   www.hostelsantafe.com;   1412 Cerrillos Rd; dm $18, r $25-35; P@⊛) This not-for-profit hostel, in a disheveled former motel, is in reach of South Capitol Rail Runner station. Three bare-bones rooms hold six-bed dorms, the rest have private or shared bathrooms. The communal lounge and kitchen make it easy to meet other travelers and get travel tips from staff, and there's a weekly donation of free food. Cash only, short daily chores required.

**Rancheros de Santa Fe
Campground**   Campground $

(☎505-466-3482;   www.rancheros.com; 736 Old Las Vegas Hwy; tent/RV sites/ cabins $25/42/49; ☉mid-Mar–Oct; ⊛⊛⊛) Eight miles southeast of the Plaza, off I-25 exit 290, Rancheros has shady, spacious sites for tents and RVs, plus simple forest cabins, nice views, a convenience store and free wi-fi. Enjoy hot showers, cheap morning coffee and evening movies.

El Paradero   B&B $$

(☎505-988-1177;   www.elparadero.com; 220 W Manhattan Ave; r from $130; P✳@⊛) Each room in this 200-year-old adobe B&B, south of the river, is unique and loaded with character. Two have their own bathrooms across the hall, the rest are en suite; our favorites are rooms 6 and 12. The full breakfasts satisfy, and rates also include afternoon tea. A separate casita holds two kitchenette suites that can be combined into one ($350).

El Rey Inn   Hotel $$

(☎505-982-1931;   www.elreyinnsantafe.com; 1862 Cerrillos Rd; r from $105; P✳@⊛⊛) This classic courtyard hotel is highly recommended, thanks to its super, Southwestern-themed rooms and suites, scattered through 5 acres of landscaped gardens. Some rooms have kitchenettes, and the sizable outdoor pool has a hot tub alongside.

La Fonda   Historic Hotel $$$

(☎800-523-5002;   www.lafondasantafe.com; 100 E San Francisco St; r/ste from $219/309; P✳@⊛⊛) Long renowned as the 'Inn at the end of the Santa Fe Trail,' Santa Fe's loveliest historic hotel sprawls through an old adobe just off the Plaza. Recently upgraded while retaining its beautiful folk-art windows and murals, it's both classy and cozy, with some wonderful top-floor luxury suites, and superb sunset views from the rooftop Bell Tower Bar.

Inn of the Five Graces
Boutique Hotel $$$

(☑505-992-0957; www.fivegraces.com; 150 E DeVargas St; ste $450-800; P ❄ 🐾) Much more than just another luxury getaway, this exquisite, one-of-a-kind gem offers an upscale gypsy-style escape. Sumptuous suites are decorated in a lavish Persian/Indian/Asian fusion theme, with fireplaces, beautifully tiled kitchenettes and a courtyard behind river-rock walls. The Luminaria House ($2500 per night) has two master bedrooms, five fireplaces and all the opulence you'd expect for the price.

Ten Thousand Waves
Resort $$$

(☑505-982-9304; www.tenthousand waves.com; 3451 Hyde Park Rd; r from $239; P ❄ 🐾 🐾) This Japanese spa resort, 4 miles northeast of the Plaza, features 13 gorgeous, Zen-inspired freestanding guesthouses. Most come with fireplaces and either a deck or courtyard, and all are within walking distance of the mountainside hot tubs and massage cabins. Pets are welcomed – for $20 extra – with custom-size beds, bones and treats.

- - - - - - - - - - - - - - - - - -

✕ Eating

Santa Fe Baking Company
American $

(☑505-988-4292; www.santafebakingcompanycafe. com; 504 W Cordova Rd; mains $6-12; ⊘6am-8pm Mon-Sat, to 6pm Sun; 🐾🐾🐾) This bustling cafe, serving burgers, sandwiches and big breakfast platters – and smoothies – all day epitomizes the human melting pot that is Santa Fe. Need proof? Local radio station KSFR broadcasts a talk show from here at 8am on weekdays.

Tia Sophia's
New Mexican $

(☑505-983-9880; 210 W San Francisco St; mains $7-10; ⊘7am-2pm Mon-Sat, 8am-1pm Sun; 🐾🐾) Local artists and visiting celebrities outnumber tourists at this longstanding and always packed Santa Fe favorite. Breakfast is the meal of choice, with fantastic burritos and other Southwestern dishes, but lunch is pretty damn tasty too; try the perfectly prepared *chile rellenos* (stuffed chile peppers), or the rota of daily specials. The shelf of kids' books helps little ones pass the time.

Jambo Cafe
African $$

(☑505-473-1269; www.jambocafe.net; 2010 Cerrillos Rd; mains $9-16; ⊘11am-9pm Mon-Sat) Despite expanding year on year, this African-flavored cafe is hard to spot from the highway; once inside, though, it's a lovely spot, always busy with locals who love its distinctive goat, chicken and lentil curries, veggie sandwiches and roti flatbreads, not to mention the reggae soundtrack.

Harry's Roadhouse
American, New Mexican $$

(☑505-989-4629; www.harrysroadhousesanta fe. com; 96 Old Las Vegas Hwy; breakfast $6-10, lunch $8-11, dinner $8-22; ⊘7am-9:30pm; 🐾) This casual longtime favorite on the southern edge of town feels like a rambling cottage with its various rooms and patio garden – and there's also a full bar. And, seriously, *everything* here is good. Especially the desserts.

Tune-Up Cafe
International $$

(☑505-983-7060; www.tuneupsantafe.com; 1115 Hickox St; mains $8-15; ⊘7am-10pm Mon-Fri, from 8am Sat & Sun; 🐾) Casual neighborhood hangout, west of the Railyard, where the chef, from El Salvador, adds his own twists to classic New Mexican and American brunch favorites while also serving fantastic Salvadoran *pupusas* (stuffed corn tortillas), *molé colorado* enchiladas and fish tacos.

Decorative pottery, Santa Fe
GLOW IMAGES, INC / GETTY IMAGES ©

Tesuque Village Market
Cafe $$

(☑505-988-8848; www.tesuquevillagemarket. com; 138 Tesuque Village Rd, Tesuque; mains $9-24; ⊙7am-9pm) Hole-in-the-wall turned country-hip, this is a weekend hotspot for folks heading to or from Tesuque Flea Market. If you're hungry and in a hurry, grab a handheld burrito – the breakfast burritos will start your day right, and the *carne adovada* (stewed pork with red chile) is among the best anywhere. Take Bishops Lodge Rd or Hwy 285 north to exit 168.

Cowgirl Hall of Fame
Barbecue $$

(☑505-982-2565; www.cowgirlsantafe.com; 319 S Guadalupe St; mains $8-23; ⊙11:30am-midnight Mon-Thu, 11am-1am Fri & Sat, 11am-11:30pm Sun; ⊛) With its juicy barbecue, awesome margaritas, outside patio, billiard room and live music – and its exuberant celebration of the women who made the West – this restaurant-bar is a fun place for all ages; there's even a kids' playground out back. Be sure to try the barbecue brisket, say in a quesadilla with red chile.

La Plazuela
New Mexican $$$

(☑505-982-5511; www.lafondasantafe.com; 100 E San Francisco St, La Fonda de Santa Fe; lunch $11-18, dinner $14-32; ⊙7am-2pm & 5-10pm Mon-Fri, 7am-3pm & 5-10pm Sat & Sun) One of Santa Fe's greatest pleasures is a meal in the Fonda's irresistible see-and-be-seen central atrium, with its excited bustle, colorful decor and high-class New Mexican food, with contemporary dishes sharing menu space with standards like fajitas and tamales.

El Farol
Tapas, Spanish $$$

(☑505-983-9912; www.elfarolsf.com; 808 Canyon Rd; lunch $8-18, dinner $25-35; ⊙11:30am-late; ☑⊛) This popular restaurant and bar, set in a rustically authentic adobe, has live music nightly. Although El Farol serves excellent steaks, most people come to sample the extensive list of tapas (three for $25). The weekly $25 flamenco dinner show and other entertainment (usually starting at 8pm) is perfect for special occasions. Kids will also dig it.

Cafe Pasqual's
International $$$

(☑505-983-9340; www.pasquals.com; 121 Don Gaspar Ave; breakfast & lunch $9-16, dinner $24-43; ⊙8am-3pm & 5:30-9:30pm Sun-Thu, to 10pm Fri & Sat; ☑⊛) Whatever time you visit this exuberantly colorful, utterly unpretentious place, the food, most of which has a definite south-of-the-border flavor, is worth every penny of the high prices. The breakfast menu is famous for dishes like *huevos motuleños,* made with sautéed bananas, feta cheese and more; later on, the meat and fish mains are superb. Reservations taken for dinner only.

🍷 Drinking

Talk to 10 residents and you'll get 10 different opinions about where to find the best margarita. You may have to sample the lot to decide for yourself. Similarly, Santa Feans take their tea and coffee seriously, too; the cafes that last here know what they're brewing.

The Teahouse
Cafe

(☑505-992-0972; www.teahousesantafe.com; 821 Canyon Rd; ⊙9am-9pm; 🛜) This spacious, relaxed indoor/outdoor cafe at the eastern end of Canyon Rd makes the perfect break while gallery hopping. One hundred and sixty teas from all over the world – with scones – plus a full menu (mains $11 to $16) of eggy brunch items, paninis and salads.

Evangelo's
Bar

(200 W San Francisco St; ⊙noon-1:30am Mon-Sat, to midnight Sun) Everyone is welcome in this casual, rowdy, cash-only joint, owned by the Klonis family since 1971 (ask owner-bartender Nick about his father's unusual fame). Drop in, put on some Patsy Cline and grab a draft beer – it's the perfect escape from Plaza culture. Live Goth and alternative bands perform downstairs in the appropriately named Underground.

Bell Tower Bar
Bar

(100 E San Francisco St; ⊙3pm-sunset Mon-Thu, 2pm-sunset Fri-Sun May-Oct, closed Nov-Apr) In summer this bar atop La Fonda hotel is the premier spot to catch one of those patented New Mexican sunsets while sipping a killer margarita. After dark, retire to the hotel's lobby Fiesta Bar for live country or folk music.

☆ Entertainment

Performing Arts

Opera, chamber music, performance and visual arts draw patrons from the world's most glittering cities to Santa Fe in July and August. The opera may be the belle of the ball – clad in sparkling denim – but there are lots of other highbrow and lowbrow happenings every week. Let the exhaustive online Event Calendar (www.santafe.com/calendar) become your new best friend.

Santa Fe Opera — Opera

(☑505-986-5900; www.santafeopera.org; Hwy 84/285, Tesuque; tickets $32-254, backstage tours adult/child $5/free; ⊘ Jun-Aug, backstage tours 9am Mon-Fri Jun-Aug) Many visitors flock to Santa Fe for the opera alone: the theater is a marvel, with 360-degree views of sandstone wilderness crowned with sunsets and moonrises, while at center stage the world's finest talent performs magnificent masterworks. It's still the Wild West, though; you can even wear jeans. Shuttles run to and from Santa Fe and Albuquerque; reserve online.

Lensic Performing Arts Center — Performing Arts

(☑505-988-7050; www.lensic.com; 211 W San Francisco St) A beautifully renovated 1930 movie house, the theater hosts touring productions and classic films as well as seven different performance groups, including the Santa Fe Symphony Orchestra & Chorus.

Live Music & Dance Clubs

Many of the hotel bars in Santa Fe offer live music on one or more nights of the week. Check the *Santa Fe Reporter* and Friday's

SANTA FE GALLERY-HOPPING

Originally a Pueblo Indian footpath, later the main street through a Spanish farming community, Santa Fe's most famous art avenue, Canyon Road (www.canyon roadarts.com), embarked on its current incarnation in the 1920s, when artists led by Los Cinco Pintores (five painters who fell in love with New Mexico's landscape) moved in to take advantage of the cheap rent.

Today Canyon Rd is a must-see attraction, holding more than a hundred of Santa Fe's 300-plus galleries. The epicenter of the city's vibrant art scene, it offers everything from rare Native American antiquities to Santa Fe School masterpieces and in-your-face modern work. If gallery-hopping seems a bit overwhelming, don't worry, just wander.

Friday nights are particularly fun: that's when the galleries put on glittering openings, starting around 5pm. Not only are these great social events, but you can also browse while nibbling on cheese, sipping Chardonnay or sparkling cider, and chatting with the artists.

Below is just a sampling of our Canyon Rd (and around) favorites. For more, pick up the handy, free *Collector's Guide* map, or check out www.santafegalleries.net. Further galleries are concentrated around the Railyard, and along Lincoln Ave just north of the Plaza.

LoneDog NoiseCat (☑505-412-1797; www.lonedognoisecat.com; 241 Delgado St; ⊘10am-4pm) Exactly the kind of gallery first-timers hope to find along Canyon Rd, and until now seldom did – a provocative and stimulating array of proudly contemporary Native American (or 'Neo-Aboriginal') art, eschewing stereotypes in favor of confronting modern realities, and curated by artists Ed Archie NoiseCat and Todd LoneDog Bordeaux.

Adobe Gallery (☑505-955-0550; www.adobegallery.com; 221 Canyon Rd; ⊘10am-5pm Mon-Sat) This gallery specializes in exquisite 20th-century ceramic pieces from the Pueblo pottery renaissance, and also sells rugs, kachinas and other artifacts produced by Southwestern Indian artisans.

Economos/Hampton Galleries (☑505-982-6347; 500 Canyon Rd; ⊘10am-5pm Mon-Sat) Museums come here to purchase superlative ancient Native American art, pre–Columbian Mexican pieces and much, much more, crammed into two huge floors swirling with history.

GF Contemporary (☑505-983-3707; www.gfcontemporary.com; 707 Canyon Rd; ⊘10am-5pm) An eclectic and well displayed assortment of modern paintings and sculpture, few of which have any overt Southwestern connection.

Navajo children, Gallup

New Mexican for a thorough listing of what's going on – clubs here change faster than the seasons.

El Farol — Dinner Show

(☑ 505-983-9912; www.elfarolsf.com; 808 Canyon Rd; dinner shows $25; ☉ 11am-midnight Mon-Sat, 11am-11pm Sun) Aside from its weekly flamenco dinner shows, this popular restaurant/bar programs live entertainment every night, including regular Latin soul shows.

Warehouse 21 — Live Music

(☑ 505-989-4423; www.warehouse21.org; 1614 Paseo de Peralta) This all-ages club and arts center in a 3500-sq-ft warehouse by the Railyard is the perfect alcohol-free venue for edgy local bands, plus a fair number of nationally known acts, or for just showing off the latest in multihued hairstyles.

Shopping

Besides the Native American jewelry sold directly by the artists under the Plaza *portales,* Santa Fe holds enough shops for you to spend weeks browsing and buying. Many venues combine both gallery and shop. The focus is mainly on art, from jewelry to wild contemporary paintings.

Seret & Sons — Handicrafts

(☑ 505-988-9151; www.seretandsons.com; 224 Galisteo St) Feel like you've stepped into an Arabian bazaar at this emporium of art and sculpture, overflowing with gorgeous Afghan rugs, Tibetan furniture, giant stone elephants and solid teak doors. Getting such treasures home is easier said than done, but it's fun just to browse too.

Santa Fe Farmers Market — Market

(☑ 505-983-4098; www.santafefarmersmarket.com; Paseo de Peralta & Guadalupe St; ☉ 8am-1pm Sat, plus Tue May-Nov; ⛟) Local produce, much of it heirloom and organic, is on sale at this spacious indoor/outdoor market, alongside homemade goodies, inexpensive food, natural body products and arts and crafts.

ℹ️ Information

New Mexico Visitor Information Center
(☑ 505-827-7336; www.newmexico.org; 491 Old Santa Fe Trail; ☉ 8am-5pm Mon-Fri, 8am-4pm Sat & Sun) Housed in the historic 1878 Lamy Building, this friendly place offers helpful advice – and free coffee.

Public Lands Information Center (☑ 505-954-2002; www.publiclands.org; 301 Dinosaur Trail; ☉ 8:30am-4pm Mon-Fri) Staff at this hugely helpful office have maps and information on public lands throughout New Mexico, and can talk you through hiking options.

Santa Fe CVB (☑ 505-955-6200; www.santafe.org; 201 W Marcy St; ☉ 8am-5pm Mon-Fri) The bricks-and-mortar office, at the Sweeny Convention Center, offers little you won't find on the website.

Gallup

The mother town on New Mexico's Mother Road seems stuck in time. Settled in 1881, when the railroad came to town, Gallup had its heyday during the 1950s, and many of its dilapidated old motels, pawn shops and billboards have barely changed since the Eisenhower administration.

Just outside the Navajo reservation, modern-day Gallup is an interesting mix of Anglos and Native Americans. Tourism is limited mostly to Route 66 road-trippers and those in search of Native American history. Even with visitors, it's not exactly crowded, and at night it turns downright quiet.

Gallup has started to capitalize on its outdoor attractions, and a growing number of rock climbers and mountain bikers come to challenge their bodies on surrounding sandstone buttes and red mesa tops.

⊙ Sights

Local Native Americans perform social Indian dances at 7pm nightly from late June to early September at the McKinley County Courthouse (231 W Coal Ave).

Historic District   Neighborhood

Route 66, the 'main street of America,' runs straight through downtown Gallup's historic district, lined with pretty, renovated, light-red sandstone buildings housing kitschy souvenir shops and galleries selling Native American arts and crafts. A brochure available at the visitor center details around 20 noteworthy structures, built along 1st, 2nd and 3rd Sts between 1895 and 1938. They include the small Rex Museum (☑ 505-863-1363; 300 W Rte 66; admission by donation; ⊙ 8:30am-3:30pm Mon-Fri), displaying historical artifacts in a former hotel.

El Morro Theatre   Theater

(☑ 505-726-0050; www.elmorrotheatre.com; 207 W Coal Ave) Downtown Gallup's centerpiece is this beautifully restored Spanish Colonial-style theater, which originally opened in 1928. As well as live theater, music and dance, it hosts movies and children's programs.

Gallup Cultural Center   Cultural Building

(www.southwestindian.com; 218 E Rte 66; ⊙ 8am-5pm) This cultural center houses a good little museum of Indian art, including excellent collections of kachina dolls both new and old, plus pottery, sand painting and weaving. A 10ft-tall bronze sculpture of a Navajo code-talker honors the sacrifices made by Navajo men in WWII. A tiny theater screens films about Chaco and the Four Corners region. In summer, traditional dances are held nightly at 7pm.

🏃 Activities

Gallup Mural Walk   Walk
See p31.

Red Rock Park   Outdoors

(☑ 505-722-3839; ⊙ park 24hr, museum 8am-4pm Mon-Fri) Gallup is becoming known as the kind of outdoors town where those who wish to can still get lost on the bike trails. Hikers should head 6 miles east to this beautiful park, which holds a little museum and trading post with modern and traditional Indian crafts, a campground and hiking trails. The 3-mile round-trip Pyramid Rock trail leads past amazing rock formations, with 50-mile views – on clear days – from the 7487ft summit.

🛏 Sleeping

Chain and independent motels cluster just off I-40 at the edge of Gallup. Only a few of the 1950s motor lodges in town are still open, and most of those are pretty dodgy. Room rates double during Ceremonial week and other big events.

Red Rock Park Campground   Campground $

(☑ 505-722-3839; Churchrock, off Hwy 66; tent/RV sites $17/20; 🐕) Pop your tent up in this beautiful setting with easy access to tons of hiking trails. Six miles east of town, it has showers, flush toilets, drinking water and a grocery store.

El Rancho   Historic Hotel $$

(☑ 505-863-9311; www.elranchohotel.com; 1000 E Hwy 66; r from $102; P ❄ 🛜 🏊) Opened in 1937, with a superb lobby resembling a rustic hunting lodge, Gallup's finest historic hotel quickly became known as the 'home of the movie stars.' Big, bright and decorated with eclectic Old West fashions, rooms are named after former guests like Humphrey Bogart and John Wayne. There's also a good restaurant and bar, plus a cheaper, modern motel wing.

✕ Eating & Drinking

Many restaurants in Gallup do not serve liquor, so choose carefully if you want to have beer with dinner.

Coffee House   Cafe **$**

(☑505-726-0291; 203 W Coal Ave; mains $4-10; ⊙7am-8:30pm Mon-Sat) With local art on the walls and casual simplicity infusing the space, this is Gallup's quintessential coffee shop. Soups, sandwiches, pastries – all good.

Genaro's Cafe   Mexican **$**

(☑505-863-6761; www.genarosrestaurant.com; 600 W Hill Ave; mains $7-15; ⊙10:30am-7:30pm Tue-Sat) Smart Mexican restaurant, three blocks up from Route 66, serving large portions of food but no alcohol. If you like your chile hot, you'll feel right at home here, just like the rest of Gallup – this place can get crowded.

El Rancho Restaurant   American **$$**

(☑505-863-9311; 1000 E Hwy 66; breakfast & lunch $6-14, dinner $9-24; ⊙6:30am-10pm; ⓘ) Western-themed restaurant serving good steaks, burgers and salads. Dishes are named for movie stars, on a decidedly pre-feminist menu where 'leading ladies' like Lucille Ball are assigned fruit and cottage cheese while the boys get to sink their teeth into hunks of beef. The adjoining 49ers Lounge offers drinks in an Old West setting and live music once a month.

Earl's Family Restaurant   Diner **$$**

(☑505-863-4201; 1400 E Hwy 66; mains $8-17; ⊙6am-9pm Mon-Sat, from 7am Sun; ⓘ) The name says it all – Earl's is a great place to bring the kids. Fast food and dinerlike, it has been serving great green chile and fried chicken (but no alcohol) since the late 1940s, and is always packed on weekends. You may even get some shopping done: Navajo vendors sell goods to passing tourists.

🛍 Shopping

Gallup serves as the Navajo and Zuni peoples' major trading center, and is arguably the best place in New Mexico to buy top-quality goods at fair prices. Many trading posts are located in the historic downtown.

Ellis Tanner Trading Company   Arts & Crafts

(☑505-863-4434; www.etanner.com; 1980 Hwy 602; ⊙8am-7pm Mon-Sat) Just south of town toward Zuni, this long-established store,

run by a fourth-generation trader, sells everything from rugs and jewelry to hardware and groceries. Be sure to check out the pawn shop.

ⓘ Information

Gallup Visitor Information Center (☑505-727-4440; www.gallupnm.org; 201 E Rte 66; ⊙8:30am-5pm Mon-Fri) Grab a copy of the annual, full-color Gallup visitors guide.

ARIZONA

Arizona is made for road trips. Yes, the state has its showstoppers – Monument Valley, the Grand Canyon, Cathedral Rock – but it's the drives between these icons and others that really breathe life and context into a trip. For a dose of mom-and-pop friendliness, follow Route 66 into Flagstaff. To understand the sheer will of Arizona's mining barons, take a twisting drive through rugged Jerome. Native American history becomes contemporary as you drive past the inhabitants of a mesa-top Hopi village dating back 1000 years.

Controversies about hot-button issues – immigration, gay rights – have grabbed headlines recently, but these legislative issues are perhaps best left to the politicians, here only temporarily. The majestic beauty of the Grand Canyon, the saguaro-dotted deserts of Tucson, the sunset glow of Camelback Mountain and the red rocks of Sedona...they're here for the duration.

Petrified Forest National Park

The 'trees' of the Petrified Forest are fragmented, fossilized logs scattered over a vast area of semidesert grassland. Sounds boring? Not so! First, many are huge – up to 6ft in diameter – and at least one spans a ravine to form a natural bridge. Second, they're beautiful up close, with extravagantly patterned cross-sections of wood shimmering in ethereal pinks, blues and greens. And finally, they're ancient: 225 million years old, making them contemporaries of the first dinosaurs that leapt onto the scene in the Late Triassic period.

The trees arrived via major floods, only to be buried beneath silica-rich volcanic ash before they could decompose. Groundwater dissolved the silica, carried it through the logs and then crystallized into solid, sparkly quartz mashed up with iron, carbon, manganese and other minerals. Uplift and erosion eventually exposed the logs. Souvenir hunters filched thousands of tons of petrified wood before Teddy Roosevelt made the forest a national monument in 1906 (it became a national park in 1962). Scavenge today and you'll be looking at fines and even jail time.

Aside from the logs, the park also encompasses Native American ruins and petroglyphs, plus an especially spectacular section of the Painted Desert north of the I-40. Petrified Forest National Park (☑ 928-524-6228; www.nps.gov/pefo; vehicle/walk-in, bicycle & motorcycle $10/5; ☉ scenic drive 7am-8pm Jun & Jul, shorter hours Aug-May), which straddles the I-40, has an entrance at exit 311 off I-40 in the north and another off Hwy 180 in the south. A 28-mile paved scenic road links the two. To avoid backtracking, westbound travelers should start in the north, eastbound ones in the south.

A video describing how the logs were fossilized runs regularly at the Painted Desert Visitor Center (☉ 8am-5pm) near the north entrance, and the Rainbow Forest Museum (☉ 8am-7pm) near the South Entrance. Both have bookstores, park exhibits and rangers that hand out free maps and information pamphlets.

Just north of I-40 is a Route 66 interpretive marker, where you'll find a map of the whole Mother Road. Further north you'll have sweeping views of the Painted Desert, where nature presents a hauntingly beautiful palette, especially at sunset. The most mesmerizing views are from Kachina Point behind the Painted Desert Inn (admission free; ☉ 9am-5pm year-round) FREE, an old adobe turned museum adorned with impressive Hopi murals.

Kachina Point is also the trailhead for wilderness hiking and camping. There are no developed trails, water sources or food, so come prepared. Overnight camping requires a free permit available at the visitor centers.

There are no accommodations within the park and food service is limited to snacks available at the visitor centers. The closest lodging is in Holbrook.

Holbrook & Around

In the 1880s Holbrook may have been one of the wickedest towns in the Old West ('too tough for women and churches'), but today this collection of rock shops and gas stations is better known as the Route 66 town with the wacky Wigwam Motel. It's also a convenient base for exploring Petrified Forest National Park and its fossilized wood.

East of Holbrook, Route 66 barrels on as I-40 for 70 miles before entering New Mexico just beyond Lupton. The only attraction to break the monotony of the road is the section cutting through the Painted Desert in Petrified Forest National Park.

The most interesting attraction in Holbrook is the Wigwam Motel (☑ 928-524-3048; www.galerie-kokopelli.com/wigwam; 811 W Hopi Dr; r $56-62; ✱) on Route 66, where each room is its own concrete tipi. Rooms are outfitted with restored 1950s hickory log-pole furniture and retro TVs. It's a fun place to stay or snap a photo. The 1898 county courthouse is home to Holbrook's chamber of commerce and visitor center as well as the Navajo County Historical Museum (☑ 928-524-6558; 100 E Arizona St; donations appreciated; ☉ 8am-5pm Mon-Fri, 8am-4pm Sat & Sun), an eclectic assortment of historic local exhibits, including a creepy old jail. If you want to buy petrified wood or other rocks and minerals, visit Jim Gray's Petrified Wood Co (☑ 928-524-1842; www.petrifiedwoodco.com; cnr Hwys 77 & 180; ☉ 7am-7pm), an expansive complex about a mile south of town. Chain hotels are spaced along the northern part of Navajo Blvd. Along the same strip is Mesa Italiana (☑ 928-524-6696; 2318 E Navajo Blvd; mains $12-19; ☉ 11am-2pm Mon-Fri, 4-9pm daily), a busy Italian place serving pasta and pizzas.

Winslow

- - - - - - - - - - - - - - - - - - - -

⊙ Sights & Activities

Homolovi State Park   Park

(☑ 928-289-4106; http://azstateparks.com; per vehicle $7; ☉ visitor center 8am-5pm) Closed in 2010 during the state budget crisis, this grasslands park beside the Little Colorado River re-opened in 2011 with a renewed commitment to protect the artifacts and structures within this sacred Hopi ancestral homeland. Before the area was converted into a park in 1993, bold thieves used backhoes to remove artifacts. Today, short hikes lead to petroglyphs and partly excavated ancient Native American sites.

The park is 3 miles northeast of Winslow via Hwy 87 (exit 257).

🛏 Sleeping & Eating

Winslow is a handy base for the Hopi Reservation, some 60 miles northeast of here. There are plenty of chain hotels and restaurants off I-40 at exit 253.

Homolovi State Park
Campground Camping $

(📞520-586-2283; http://azstateparks.com; tent & RV sites $15-25) There's a campground with electric hookups, water and showers near the Homolovi ruins. Reserve a campsite online or by phone.

La Posada Historic Hotel $$

(📞928-289-4366; www.laposada.org; 303 E 2nd St; r $139-169; ⚙🛜🐾) An impressively restored 1930 hacienda designed by star architect du jour Mary Jane Colter, this was the last great railroad hotel built for the Fred Harvey Company along the Santa Fe Railroad. Elaborate tilework, glass-and-tin chandeliers, Navajo rugs and other details accent its palatial Western-style elegance.

They go surprisingly well with the splashy canvases of Tina Mion, one of the three preservation-minded artists who bought the rundown place in 1997. The period-styled rooms are named for illustrious former guests, including Albert Einstein, Gary Cooper and Diane Keaton. Pet fee is $10 per visit.

Turquoise Room Southwestern $$$

(www.theturquoiseroom.net; La Posada; breakfast $8-12, lunch $10-13, dinner $19-42; ⊘7am-4pm & 5-9pm) Even if you're not staying at La Posada, treat yourself to the best meal between Flagstaff and Albuquerque at this unique restaurant. Dishes have a neo-Southwestern flair, the placemats are handpainted works of art and there's a children's menu as well. If the fried squash blossoms are on the appetizer menu, toast your good fortune and order up.

❶ Information

The **visitor center** (📞928-289-2434; www.winslowarizona.org; 523 W 2nd St; ⊘9am-5pm Mon-Fri, 9am-3pm Sat) can be found inside the recently renovated Lorenzo Hubbell Trading Post.

Walnut Canyon National Monument

The Sinagua cliff dwellings at Walnut Canyon (📞928-526-3367; www.nps.gov/waca;

7-day admission adult/child $5/free; ⊘8am-5pm mid-May–Oct, 9am-5pm Nov–mid-May) are set in the nearly vertical walls of a small limestone butte amid this forested canyon. The mile-long Island Trail steeply descends 185ft (more than 200 stairs), passing 25 rooms built under the natural overhangs of the curvaceous butte. A shorter, wheelchair-accessible Rim Trail affords several views of the cliff dwelling from across the canyon. Even if you're not all that interested in the Sinagua people, who abandoned the site about 700 years ago, Walnut Canyon itself is a beautiful place to visit, not so far from Flagstaff.

Flagstaff

Flagstaff's laid-back charms are countless, from its pedestrian-friendly historic downtown crammed with eclectic vernacular architecture and vintage neon, to its high-altitude pursuits like skiing and hiking. Buskers play bluegrass on street corners while bike culture flourishes. Locals are a happy, athletic bunch, skewing more toward granola than gunslinger. Northern Arizona University (NAU) gives Flag its college-town flavor, while its railroad history still figures firmly in the town's identity. Throw in a healthy appreciation for craft beer, freshly roasted coffee beans and an all-around good time and you have the makings of the perfect outdoor town.

Approaching Flagstaff from the east, I-40 parallels Old Route 66. Their paths diverge at Enterprise Rd: I-40 veers southwest, while Old Route 66 curls northwest, hugging the railroad tracks, and is the main drag through the historic downtown. NAU sits between downtown and I-40. From downtown, I-17 heads south toward Phoenix, splitting off at Hwy 89A (also known as Alt 89), a spectacularly scenic road through Oak Creek Canyon to Sedona. Hwy 180 is the most direct route northwest to Tusayan and the South Rim (80 miles), while Hwy 89 beelines north to Cameron (59 miles), where it meets Hwy 64 heading west to the canyon's East Entrance.

◉ Sights

With its wonderful mix of cultural sites, historic downtown and access to outdoorsy pursuits, it's hard not to fall for Flagstaff.

Museum of Northern Arizona Museum

(📞928-774-5213; www.musnaz.org; 3101 N Fort Valley Rd; adult/child 10-17yr/senior $10/6/9; ⊘10am-5pm

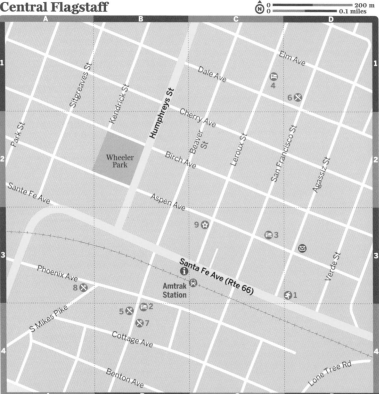

Central Flagstaff

🗿 Activities, Courses & Tours

1 Absolute Bikes D3

🛏 Sleeping

2 Dubeau Hostel B4
3 Hotel Monte Vista C3
4 Inn at 410 .... C1

🍴 Eating

5 Beaver Street Brewery B4
6 Brix D1
7 Pizzicletta A3
8 Macy's B4

🎭 Entertainment

9 Charly's Pub & Grill C3

Mon-Sat, noon-5pm Sun) Before venturing across the Colorado Plateau, introduce yourself to the region at this small but excellent museum that spotlights local Native American archaeology, history and culture, as well as geology, biology and the arts. Don't miss the extensive collection of Hopi kachina (also spelled katsina) dolls and a wonderful variety of Native American basketry and ceramics.

**Riordan Mansion State
Historic Park**   Historic Site
See p34.

Lowell Observatory ·   Observatory
(📞 main phone 928-774-3358, recorded information 928-233-3211; www.lowell.edu; 1400 W Mars Hill Rd; adult/child 5-17yr $12/6; ⌚ 9am-10pm Jun-Aug, shorter hours Sep-May) Sitting atop a hill just west of downtown, this national historic landmark was built by Percival Lowell in 1894. The first sighting of Pluto occurred here in 1930. Weather permitting, visitors can stargaze through on-site telescopes, including the famed Clark Telescope (closed

for renovations through mid-2015). This 1896 telescope was the impetus behind the now-accepted theory of an expanding universe.

The paved Pluto Walk climbs through a scale model of our solar system. Evening programming includes a video about the making of the new, seven-story Discovery Channel Telescope, which is located 40 miles southeast of Flagstaff.

☩ Activities

Scores of hiking and mountain-biking trails are easily accessed in and around Flagstaff. More than 50 miles of trails crisscross the city as part of the Flagstaff Urban Trail System (FUTS; www.flagstaff.az.gov); trail maps are available online or at the visitor center.

Stop by the USFS Flagstaff Ranger Station (☑928-526-0866; 5075 N Hwy 89; ☺8am-4pm Mon-Fri) for information about trails in the surrounding national forest or check www.fs.fed.us. The steep 3-mile hike (one way) up 9299ft Mt Elden leads to a lookout at the top of the peak's tower. If it's locked when you get there, knock and if someone is there, you may be able to climb the stairs to the lookout.

For an inside track on the local mountain-biking scene, visit the super-friendly gearheads at Absolute Bikes (☑928-779-5969; www.absolutebikes.net; 202 E Rte 66; bike rentals per day from $39; ☺9am-7pm Mon-Fri, 9am-6pm Sat, 10am-4pm Sun Apr-Dec, shorter hours Jan-Mar).

Arizona Snowbowl   Skiing

(☑928-779-1951; www.arizonasnowbowl.com; 9300 N Snowbowl Rd, Hwy 180 & Snowbowl Rd; lift ticket adult/youth 13-18yr/child 8-12yr $59/55/35; ☺9am-4pm mid-Dec–mid-Apr) About 14 miles north of downtown, Arizona Snowbowl is small but lofty, with four lifts that service 32 ski runs between 9200ft and 11,500ft.

Arizona Snowbowl offers several trails, including the strenuous 4.5-mile one-way hike up 12,633ft Humphreys Peak, the highest point in Arizona; wear decent boots as sections of the trail cross crumbly volcanic rock. In summer, ride the chairlift (www.arizonasnowbowl.com; adult/child 8-12yr $15/10; ☺10am-4pm Fri-Sun late May–mid-Oct) at Arizona Snowbowl to 11,500ft, where you can hike, attend ranger talks and take in the desert and mountain views. Children under eight ride for free.

Flagstaff Nordic Center   Skiing

(☑928-220-0550; www.flagstaffnordiccenter.com; Mile Marker 232, Hwy 180; weekend/weekday from $18/12; ☺9am-4pm Dec-Mar) ☙ Fifteen miles north of Flagstaff, the Nordic Center offers 25 miles of groomed trails for cross-country skiing, as well as lessons and rentals. Also has snowshoe and multi-use trails. Near the Nordic Center off Hwy 180 you can ski – no permit required – across forest service land. Check with the ranger station about where to park on the fire roads.

⌂ Sleeping

If you want to walk home after visiting Flagstaff's microbreweries and its top restaurants, choose a hotel downtown. If you just want a place to crash before heading to the Grand Canyon, chain motels and hotels line S Milton Rd, Beulah Blvd and W Forest Meadows St, clustering around exit 195 off I-40.

Numerous nondescript and low-rate independent motels line Old Route 66 and the railroad tracks east of downtown (exit 198 off I-40). Check the room before you pay – some are much worse than others. For the money, you're better off at one of the hostels or historic hotels downtown.

Unlike in southern Arizona, summer is high season here.

Free dispersed camping is permitted in the national forest surrounding Flagstaff. USFS campgrounds in Oak Creek Canyon are 15 to 30 miles south of town.

Woody Mountain Campground   Campground $

(☑928-774-7727, 800-732-7986; www.woodymountaincampground.com; 2727 W Rte 66; tent/RV sites $20/31; ☺Apr-Oct; @☏❄) Relax under the pines, play horseshoes and wash your hiking clothes at the coin laundry; off I-40 at exit 191.

Flagstaff KOA   Campground $

(☑928-526-9926, 800-562-3524; www.flagstaffkoa.com; 5803 N Hwy 89; tent sites $26-34, RV sites $34-68, cabins $65, tipis $55; ☺year-round; ☏❄) This big campground lies a mile north of I-40 off exit 201, 5 miles northeast of downtown. A path leads from the campground to trails at Mt Elden. It's family friendly, with banana bike rentals, minigolf and a splash park.

Dubeau Hostel
Hostel $

(☎928-774-6731; www.grandcanyonhostel.com; 19 W Phoenix St; dm $24, r $60-68; P❄@☎) This independent hostel offers the same friendly service and clean, well-run accommodations as its sister property, Grand Canyon International Hostel. The basic rooms are like basic hotel rooms, with refrigerators and bathrooms with showers, but at half the price. Breakfast is included.

Budget Inn Flagstaff
Motel $

(☎928-774-5038; www.budgetinnflagstaff.com; 913 S Milton Rd; r $96; P❄☎) Bland name, bland exterior, but whoa. Push open the door and you'll be pleasantly surprised by the inviting, not-so-bland style of this two-story motel. Staff is welcoming and rooms come with a microwave and refrigerator. The property is centrally located between downtown and I-40 on S Milton Rd.

Inn at 410
B&B $$

(☎928-774-0088; www.inn410.com; 410 N Leroux St; r $170-220; P❄@☎) This elegant and fully renovated 1894 house offers nine spacious, beautifully decorated and themed bedrooms, each with a refrigerator and private bathroom. Many rooms have four-poster beds and views of the garden or the San Francisco Peaks. A short stroll from downtown, the inn has a shady garden with fruit trees and a cozy dining room, where the full gourmet breakfast and afternoon snacks are served.

Hotel Monte Vista
Hotel $$

(☎928-779-6971; www.hotelmontevista.com; 100 N San Francisco St; r $70-120, ste $130-150; ❄☎) A huge, old-fashioned neon sign towers over this allegedly haunted 1926 hotel, hinting at what's inside: feather lampshades, vintage furniture, bold colors and eclectic decor. Rooms are named for the movie stars who slept in them, such as the Humphrey Bogart room, with dramatic black walls, yellow ceiling and gold-satin bedding. Several resident ghosts supposedly make regular appearances. The Monte Vista's appeal comes from all of its glorious funkiness, and high-maintenance travelers not enamored of funkiness may be happier elsewhere. Four rooms have shared bathrooms.

-- -- -- -- -- -- -- -- -- -- -- -- -- -- --

✕ Eating

For groceries, **Bashas'** (☎928-774-3882; www.bashas.com; 2700 S Woodlands Village Blvd; ◷6am-

11pm) is a good local chain supermarket with a respectable selection of organic foods. For health food, try the new **Whole Foods Market** (☎928-774-5747; 320 S Cambridge Lane; ◷8am-9pm; ✈).

Macy's
Cafe $

(www.macyscoffee.net; 14 S Beaver St; mains under $8; ◷6am-8pm; ☎) The delicious house-roasted coffee at this Flagstaff institution has kept the city buzzing for more than 30 years now. The vegetarian menu includes many vegan choices, along with traditional cafe grub like pastries, steamed eggs, waffles, yogurt and granola, salads and veggie sandwiches.

Coppa Cafe
Cafe $$

(☎928-637-6813; www.coppacafe.net; 1300 S Milton Rd; lunch & brunch $9-15, dinner $21-31; ◷11am-7pm Wed & Thu, 11am-8pm Fri & Sat, 10am-4pm Sun) Brian Konefal and Paola Fioravanti are the husband-and-wife team behind this inviting cafe. The couple, who met at an Italian culinary school, whip up an enticing array of European dishes and desserts that are locally sourced and, on occasion, locally 'foraged' from nearby forests. Look for salads, seasonal quiche and shepherd's pie at lunchtime and juniper-braised wild boar and pasta alla carbonara with duck egg in the evening. With its savory fare and country-bistro decor, you'll soon forget that you've just ambled in from busy S Milton Rd.

Pizzicletta
Pizza $$

(www.pizzicletta.com; 203 W Phoenix Ave; pizzas $10-15; ◷from 5pm Tue-Sun) When the wood-fired pie is piled perfectly high – that's amore. When the crowd seems to shine like it's had too much wine – that's amore. When the train passes by like a bolt from the sky – that's amore. It's also the tiny Pizzicletta, where the thin-crusted pizzas are loaded with gourmet toppings like arugula and aged prosciutto. Ring-a-ling-a-ling, it's hard not to sing at Pizzicletta.

Beaver Street Brewery
Brewpub $$

(www.beaverstreetbrewery.com; 11 S Beaver St; lunch $8-23, dinner $13-23; ◷11am-11pm Sun-Thu, to midnight Fri & Sat; ☝) Families, river guides, ski bums and businesspeople – everybody is here or on the way. The menu is typical brewpub fare, with delicious pizzas, burgers and salads, and there's usually eight hand-crafted beers on tap, like its Railhead Red

Snow Cap Drive-In, Seligman

Ale or R&R Oatmeal Stout, plus some seasonal brews. Serious drinkers can walk next door to play pool at the 21-and-over Brews & Cues.

Brix American $$$

(📞 928-213-1021; www.brixflagstaff.com; 413 N San Francisco St; mains $23-34; ⏰ 5-9pm Sun-Thu, until 10pm Fri & Sat) Are you settled in at the bar? Inhale, look around, relax. This is your vacation reward. Brix brings a breath of fresh, unpretentious sophistication to Flagstaff's dining scene as well as easygoing but polished hospitality. The menu varies seasonally, regularly using what is fresh, ripe, local and organic for dishes like wild mushroom risotto with truffles and grilled ribeye with red onion jam.

🍷 Drinking & Nightlife

Craft beer fans can follow the Flagstaff-Grand Canyon Ale Trail (www.flagstaff aletrail.com) to sample microbrews at downtown breweries and a bar or two. Buy a trail passport at the visitor center or one of the breweries listed on the website.

For details about festivals and music programs, call the visitor center or check www.flagstaff365.com. On Saturday nights in summer, people gather on blankets for music and family movies (free) at Heritage Sq. The fun starts at 5pm.

Pick up the free *Flagstaff Live!*, published on Thursdays, or check out www.flaglive.com for current shows and happenings around town.

Museum Club Bar

(📞 928-526-9434; www.themuseumclub.com; 3404 E Rte 66; ⏰ 11am-2am) This honky-tonk roadhouse on Route 66 has been kicking up its heels since 1936. Inside what looks like a huge log cabin, you'll find a large wooden dance floor, animal mounts and a sumptuous elixir-filled mahogany bar. The origins of the name? In 1931 it housed a taxidermy museum.

Charly's Pub & Grill Live Music

(📞 928-779-1919; www.weatherfordhotel.com; 23 N Leroux St; ⏰ 8am-2am) This restaurant at the Weatherford Hotel has regular live music. Its fireplace and brick walls provide a cozy setting for the blues, jazz and folk played here. Head upstairs to stroll the wraparound veranda outside the popular 3rd-floor Zane Grey Ballroom, which overlooks the historic district.

ℹ Information

Visitor Center (📞 800-842-7293, 928-774-9541; www.flagstaffarizona.org; 1 E Rte 66; ⏰ 8am-5pm Mon-Sat, 9am-4pm Sun) Inside the Amtrak station, the visitor center has a great Flagstaff Discovery map and tons of information on things to do.

Route 66: Williams to Kingman

On the way to Kingman, Route 66 arcs north away from the I-40 for 115 dusty miles of original Mother Road through scrubby, lonely landscape. It appears briefly as Main St in Williams, then merges with the I-40 near Seligman. Gas stations are rare, so make sure you've got enough fuel. The total distance to Kingman is 130 miles.

Seligman

POP 469 / ELEV 5240FT

This tiny town embraces its Route 66 heritage with verve, thanks to the Delgadillo brothers, who for decades were the Mother Road's biggest boosters. Juan passed away in 2004, but nonagenarian Angel and his wife Vilma still run Angel's Barbershop (☑928-422-3352; www.route66giftshop.com; 217 E Rte 66; ◷9am-5pm). OK, so he doesn't cut hair anymore, but the barber's chair is still there and you can poke around for souvenirs and admire license plates sent in by fans from all over the world. If Angel is around, he's usually happy to regale you with stories about the Dust Bowl era. He's seen it all.

Angel's madcap brother Juan used to rule prankishly supreme over the Snow Cap Drive-In (☑928-422-3291; 301 E Rte 66; mains $3.25-6.25; ◷10am-6pm mid-Mar–Nov), a Route 66 institution now kept going by his sons Bob and John. The crazy decor is only the beginning. Wait until you see the menu featuring cheeseburgers with cheese and 'dead chicken!' Beware the fake mustard bottle... They sometimes open at 9am in mid-summer.

Two good restaurants stare each other down from opposite sides of Route 66. For friendly service and good American and German grub, try Westside Lilo's Cafe (415 W Rte 66; breakfast & lunch $5-14, dinner $13-21; ◷6am-9pm), which also has an outdoor patio. For beer and a few tongue-in-cheek menu items, try the Roadkill Café & OK Saloon (502 W Rte 66; breakfast $7-12, lunch & dinner $7-22; ◷7am-9pm) across the street, which has an all-you-can-eat salad bar, juicy steaks and burgers and, of course, the 'splatter platter.'

For welcoming hosts and the town's best neon sign, look no further than the Supai Motel (☑928-422-4153; www.supaimotel.com; 134 W Chino Ave; s/d $60/72; ❄🐾), a classic courtyard motel that offers simple but perfectly fine rooms complete with refrigerators and microwaves. The Havasu Falls mural is an inspiring way to start the morning.

Look out for red-and-white Burma Shave signs on the 23 miles of road slicing through rolling hills out of Seligman.

Grand Canyon Caverns

Grand Canyon Caverns & Inn

The restaurant (◷8am-6pm Jun-Oct, varies rest of year) is nice if you already happen to be here; it has a small playground and serves simple American fare. The bar opens at 3pm on Fridays and Saturdays and closes at 10pm or later depending on crowd-size. The campground (tent/RV sites $15/30) here has over 50 sites carved out of the juniper forest, plus new open-air, roof-free rooms (from $60) on raised platforms for star-gazers. The Caverns Inn (r $90; ❄🐾) has rooms that are basic but well kept. There's wi-fi in the lobby. Pets are $5 per day with a refundable $50 deposit.

Peach Springs to Kingman

It's tempting to try to race the train on this lonely stretch of Mother Road where your only other friend is the pavement unfurling for miles ahead. After passing through the blink-and-you'll-miss-them towns of Truxton and Valentine, you'll come to tiny Hackberry, where highway memorialist Robert Waldmire lures passersby with his much loved Old Route 66 Visitor Center (☑928-769-2605; www.hackberrygeneralstore.com; 11255 E Rte 66; ◷typically 8am-6pm) FREE inside an eccentrically decorated gas station. It's a refreshing spot for a cold drink and souvenirs.

Kingman

Among Route 66 aficionados, Kingman is known as the main hub of the longest uninterrupted stretch of the historic highway, running from Seligman to Topcock. Among its early 20th-century buildings is the former Methodist church at 5th and Spring St where Clark Gable and Carole Lombard wed in 1939. Hometown hero Andy Devine had his Hollywood breakthrough as the perpetually befuddled driver of the eponymous *Stagecoach* in John Ford's Oscar-winning 1939 movie.

These days, Kingman feels like a place waking up from a long nap. New eateries, watering holes and galleries have been opening on Beale St, the axis of historic downtown, adding some foot traffic and modern verve.

Route 66 barrels through town as Andy Devine Ave. It runs parallel to the up-and-coming Beale St. Supermarkets, gas stations and other businesses line up along northbound Stockton Hill Rd, which is also the road to take for Grand Canyon West.

◉ Sights & Activities

Route 66 Museum Museum

See p36.

Mohave Museum of History & Arts Museum

(☑ 928-753-3195; www.mohavemuseum.org; 400 W Beale St; adult/senior/child 12yr & under $4/3/free; ☺ 9am-5pm Mon-Fri, 1-5pm Sat) Admission to the Route 66 Museum also gets you into the Mohave Museum, a warren of rooms filled with extraordinarily eclectic stuff. All sorts of regional topics are dealt with, from mining towns to Andy Devine. There's also an entire wall of oil portraits of American first ladies – all painted by the same artist! And check out the piece of petrified lightning. Tickets can also be used at the Route 66 Museum in the Powerhouse.

Hualapai Mountain Park Park

(☑ 928-681-5700; www.mcparks.com; 6250 Hualapai Mountain Rd; day use $7) In summer locals climb this nearby mountain for picnics, hiking, mountain biking and wildlife-watching amid cool ponderosa pine and aspen.

✦ Festivals & Events

Historic Route 66 Fun Run Car Show

(☑ 928-753-5001; www.azrt66.com; ☺ May) Vintage car rally from Seligman to Topock on the first weekend in May.

⌂ Sleeping

Kingman has plenty of motels along Route 66/Andy Devine Ave north and south of the I-40. The cheapest places are dingy and popular with down-on-their-luck, long-term residents. Inspect before committing.

Hualapai Mountain Park Campground $

(☑ 928-681-5700, 877-757-0915; www.mcparks.com; Hualapai Mountain Rd; tent/RV sites $17/30, tipis $35, cabins $65-135; ☒) Camp among granite

rock formations and ponderosa pine at this pretty county park, some 15 miles south of town. The tipis are cool, but we hear they stay rather chilly in cold weather. Some cabins have restrooms and showers. Tent sites are first-come, first-served but RV sites can be reserved. Pets are $2 per pet per day; $5 reservation fee.

Hualapai Mountain Resort Lodge $

(☑ 928-757-3545; www.hmresort.net; 4525 Hualapai Mountain Rd; r $79-99, ste $159; ☒) Think mountain-man chic: chunky wood furniture, bold paintings of wild game and a front porch that's made for wildlife-watching among the towering pines. The lodge advertises wi-fi, but we were not able to get it to work. The good on-site restaurant serves breakfast, lunch and dinner Wednesday through Sunday. Try to get a table near the window to scan for elk.

Travelodge Motel $

(☑ 928-757-1188; www.travelodge.com; 3275 E Andy Devine Ave; r incl breakfast $61-81; ❋ ☎ ☒ ☒) Budget travelers, rejoice. This two-story motel provides everything you need for a satisfying overnight stay in Kingman: a Route 66–adjacent location, helpful staff, continental breakfast, refrigerator and microwaves in the room, a laundry and free wi-fi. Pet fee is $10 per pet per day.

✕ Eating & Drinking

Sirens Cafe Sandwiches $

(www.sirensinkingman.com; 419 E Beale St; sandwiches $7; ☺ 10am-4pm Mon-Fri) A mother-daughter team runs this welcoming cafe, which serves gourmet sandwiches and paninis. Desserts look nothing less than decadent.

Redneck's Southern Pit BBQ Barbecue $$

(www.redneckssouthernpitbbq.com; 420 E Beale St; mains $5.25-24; ☺ 11am-8pm Tue-Sat; ☎) As rednecks, we can confirm that the pork is darn tasty at this Beale St BBQ joint, but we're not too keen on the word 'sammiches,' which appears on the menu. 'Big old tater,' however, is fine. Also serves rib platters. Order at the counter then grab a seat. Good option for families.

Cellar Door Wine Bar

(☑ 928-753-3885; www.the-cellar-door.com; 414 E Beale St; appetizers under $8; ☺ 4-10pm Wed & Thu, 4pm-midnight Fri & Sat) This downtown wine bar offers about 140 wines by the bottle, 30 by the glass, an international selection of beers and tasty appetizer plates. It's a hot little spot that embodies the spirit of revival in Kingman.

Beale Street Brews Coffee Shop

(www.bealestreetbrews.net; 418 E Beale St; ⊙7am-3pm Mon-Thu, until 7pm Thu, until 10pm Fri & Sat; 🛜) This cute indie coffee shop draws local java cognoscenti with its lattes and gallery.

❶ Information

Powerhouse Visitor Center (📞866-427-7866, 928-753-6106; www.gokingman.com; 120 W Andy Devine Ave; ⊙8am-5pm) Lots of information about Route 66 attractions.

Topock Gorge to Oatman

Coming from California, Route 66 enters Arizona at Topock, near the 20-mile Topock Gorge, a dramatic walled canyon that's one of the prettiest sections of the Colorado River. It's part of the Havasu National Wildlife Refuge (📞760-326-3853; www.fws.gov/refuge/havasu), a major habitat for migratory and water birds. Look for herons, ducks, geese, blackbirds and other winged creatures as you raft or canoe through the gorge. There are plenty of coves and sandy beaches for picnics and sunning. Companies renting boats include Jerkwater Canoe & Kayak (📞928-768-7753; www.jerkwatercanoe.com; tours $46; ⊙launch at 7:30am PCT) which launches day trips from Park Moabi in Needles, CA, just west of the state line. Rates include canoe rental for the 17-mile float from the park to Castle Rock and the return shuttle.

North of here, in Golden Shores, you can refuel on gas and grub before embarking on a rugged 20-mile trip to the terrifically crusty former gold-mining town of Oatman, cupped by pinnacles and craggy hills. Since the veins of ore ran dry in 1942, the little settlement has reinvented itself as a movie set and unapologetic Wild West tourist trap, complete with staged gunfights (daily at noon, 1:30pm and sometimes 3:30pm) and gift stores named Fast Fanny's Place and the Classy Ass. And speaking of asses, there are plenty of them (the four-legged kind, that is) roaming the streets and shamelessly begging for food. You can buy hay squares in town. Stupid and endearing, they're descendents from pack animals left behind by the early miners.

Clark apparently returned quite frequently to play cards with the miners in the downstairs saloon, which is awash in one-dollar bills (some $40,000 worth by the barmaid's estimate). At the time of research, the upstairs, where visitors used to be able to peek into the old guest rooms, was closed for renovations. Beyond Oatman, keep your wits about you as the road twists and turns past tumbleweeds, saguaro cacti and falling rocks as it travels over Sitgreaves Pass (3523ft) and corkscrews into the rugged Black Mountains before arriving in Kingman.

Western Route 66

Starting from Needles near the Nevada stateline, Route 66 runs a gauntlet of Mojave Desert ghost towns then crosses over the Cajon Pass to the railroad towns of Victorville and Barstow. It rumbles through the LA basin and ends in beachside Santa Monica.

In California Route 66 mostly follows the National Trails Hwy, prone to potholes and dangerous bumps. In larger towns, Mother Road relics may require a careful eye amid more contemporary architecture, but as you head toward Nevada, wide open vistas and the occasional landmark remain barely changed from the days of the original Route 66 road trippers.

Note that the destination content here follows Route 66 across California from west to east, in reverse from the road trip found on page 39.

LOS ANGELES

LA runs deeper than her blonde beaches, bosomy hills and ubiquitous beemers would have you believe. She's a myth. A beacon for countless small-town dreamers, rockers and risk-takers, an open-minded angel who encourages her people to live and let live without judgment or shame. She has given us Quentin Tarantino, Jim Morrison and Serena and Venus Williams, spawned skateboarding and gangsta rap, popularized implants, electrolysis and Spandex, and has nurtured not just great writers, performers and directors, but also the ground-breaking yogis who first brought Eastern wisdom to the Western world.

LA is best defined by those simple life-affirming moments. A cracked-ice, jazz-age cocktail on Beverly Blvd, a hike high into the Hollywood Hills sagebrush, a swirling pod of dolphins off Point Dume, a pink-washed sunset over a thundering Venice Beach drum circle, the perfect taco. And her night music. There is always night music.

Santa Monica & Venice

Here's a place where real-life Lebowskis sip white Russians next to martini-swilling Hollywood producers, and celebrity chefs and soccer moms shop shoulder to shoulder at abundant farmers markets. It's a small city with forward-thinking social and environmental ideals (and fascist parking codes) alive with surf rats, skate punks, string bikinis, yoga freaks, psychics, street performers and a prodigious homeless population. Most, if not all, of that can be found along a stretch of sublime coastline that cradles the city to the west, and laps at the heels of an undulating mountain range that defines the entire LA area to the north. This is Santa Monica – LA's hippie-chic little sister, its karmic counterbalance and, to many, its salvation.

Once the very end of the mythical Route 66, and still a tourist love affair, the Santa Monica Pier (310-458-8900; www.santamonicapier.org; west of Ocean Ave; admission free;) dates back to 1908, is stocked with rides and arcade games and blessed with spectacular views, and is the city's most compelling landmark. After a stroll on the pier, hit the beach (☎310-458-8411; http://www.smgov.net/portals/beach/; ▣BBB 1). We like the stretch just north of Ocean Park Blvd. Or rent a bike or some skates from Perry's Cafe (☎310-939-0000; www.perryscafe.com; Ocean Front Walk; mountain bikes & Rollerblades per hr/day $10/30, bodyboards per hr/day $7/17; ⊙9:30am-5:30pm) and explore the 22-mile South Bay Bicycle Trail.

The Venice Boardwalk (Ocean Front Walk; Venice Pier to Rose Ave; ⊙24hr), officially known as Ocean Front Walk, is a wacky carnival alive with altered-states hoola-hoop acrobats, old-timey jazz combos, solo distorted garage rockers and artists – good and bad, but as far as LA experiences go, it's a must. Rent a bike (☎310-396-2453; 517 Ocean Front Walk; per hr/2hr/day bikes $7/12/20, surfboards $10/20/30, skates $7/12/20) and join the parade, glimpse Muscle Beach (www.musclebeach.net; 1800 Ocean Front Walk; per day $10; ⊙8am-7pm May-Sep, to 6pm Oct-Apr) or hit the Skate Park (1800 Ocean Front Walk; ⊙dawn-dusk). The Sunday afternoon drum circle is always wild.

🛏 Sleeping

HI Los Angeles-Santa Monica   Hostel $
(☎310-393-9913; www.hilosangeles.org; 1436 2nd St; dm $38-49, r $99-159; ✳@⊛) Near the beach and promenade, this hostel has an enviable location on the cheap. Its 200 beds in single-sex dorms and bed-in-a-box doubles with shared bathrooms are clean and safe, and

there are plenty of public spaces to lounge and surf, but those looking to party are better off in Venice or Hollywood.

Palihouse   Boutique Hotel $$$
(☎310-394-1279; www.palihousesantamonica.com; 1001 3rd St; r $279-319, studios $319-379; ℗✳@⊛) LA's grooviest new hotel brand (not named Ace) has taken over the 36 rooms, studios and one-bedroom apartments of the historic Embassy Hotel (c 1927). Expect a lobby with terra-cotta floors, beamed ceilings and coffee bar, plus booths and leather sofas on which you can canoodle and surf.

Shore Hotel   Hotel $$$
(☎310-458-1515; www.shorehotel.com; 1515 Ocean Ave; r from $309) Massive, clean-lined and modern, featuring wood-and-glass rooms each with private terraces, this is one of the newest hotels on Ocean Ave, and the only gold LEED-certified hotel in Santa Monica, which means it has a reasonably light footprint. Case in point: the lovely back garden is seeded with drought-tolerant plants.

🍴 Eating

Santa Monica Farmers Markets   Market $
(www.smgov.net/portals/farmersmarket; Arizona Ave, btwn 2nd & 3rd Sts; ⊙8:30am-1:30pm Wed, to 1pm Sat; ⚒) ✿ You haven't really experienced Santa Monica until you've explored one of its weekly outdoor farmers markets stocked

VERITY E MILLIGAN / GETTY IMAGES ©

Santa Monica Pier

Santa Monica & Venice

0 ———————— 500 m
0 ———————— 0.25 miles

Santa Monica & Venice

◎ Sights
1 Santa Monica Pier A3
2 Santa Monica State Beach A2

✦ Activities, Courses & Tours
3 Muscle Beach A6
4 Perry's Café & Rentals A2

▣ Sleeping
5 HI Los Angeles-Santa Monica A2
6 Palihouse B1
7 Shore Hotel A2

✕ Eating
8 Bar Pintxo A2
9 Bay Cities B2
10 Santa Monica Farmers Markets B2

▣ Drinking & Nightlife
11 Basement Tavern B4
12 Misfit B2

✿ Entertainment
13 Planet Blue B5
14 Santa Monica Place B2
15 Third Street Promenade B2

with organic fruits, vegetables, flowers, baked goods and fresh-shucked oysters.

Bay Cities Deli, Italian $

(www.baycitiesitaliandeli.com; 1517 Lincoln Blvd; sandwiches $5-9; ⊙ 9am-7pm Tue-Sat, to 6pm Sun) Not just the best Italian deli in LA, this is arguably the best deli, period. With sloppy, spicy godmothers (piled with salami, mortadella, coppacola, ham, prosciutto, provolone, and pepper salad), house-roasted tri-tip, tangy salads, imported meats, cheeses, breads, oils and extras. Get your sandwich with the works. And, yes, it's worth the wait.

Milo and Olive Italian $$

(☎ 310-453-6776; www.miloandolive.com; 2723 Wilshire Blvd; dishes $7-20; ⊙ 7am-11pm) We love it for its small-batch wines, incredible pizzas and terrific breakfasts (creamy polenta and poached eggs anyone?), breads and pastries, all of which you may enjoy at the marble bar or shoulder to shoulder with new friends at one of two common tables. It's a cozy, neighborhoody kind of joint; no reservations.

Bar Pintxo
Spanish $$

(☎ 310-458-2012; www.barpintxo.com; 109 Santa Monica Blvd; tapas $4-16, paella $30; ⊙ 4-10pm Mon-Wed, to 11pm Thu, to midnight Fri, noon-midnight Sat, to 10pm Sun) A Barcelona-inspired tapas bar. It's small, it's cramped, it's a bit loud and a lot of fun. Tapas include pork belly braised in duck fat, filet mignon skewers, lamb meatballs and a tremendous seared calamari.

🍷 Drinking & Nightlife

Basement Tavern
Bar

(www.basementtavern.com; 2640 Main St; ⊙ 5pm-2am) This creative speakeasy is our favorite well in Santa Monica. We love it for its cocktails, cozy booths and nightly live-music calendar that features blues, jazz, bluegrass and rock. It gets too busy on weekends, but weeknights can be special.

Misfit
Lounge

(☎ 310-656-9800; www.themisfitbar.com; 225 Santa Monica Blvd; ⊙ noon-late Mon-Fri, from 11am Sat & Sun) This darkly lit emporium of food, drink and fun is notable for the decent – not great – menu, and phenomenal cocktails made from craftsman spirits. Set in a historic building decked out with a retro interior, it's busy from brunch to last call.

🛍 Shopping

For big chains such as Anthropologie, the flagship Apple, Guess and Converse, make your way to the Third Street Promenade. Santa Monica Place (www.santamonicaplace.com; 395 Santa Monica Pl; ⊙ 10am-9pm Mon-Thu, to 10pm Fri & Sat, 11am-8pm Sun) offers more upscale corporate consumption. For indie-minded boutiques, such as Planet Blue (www.shopplanetblue.com; 2940 Main St; ⊙ 10am-6pm), head to Montana Ave and Main St.

ℹ Information

Santa Monica (☎ 800-544-5319; www.santamonica.com; 2427 Main St) Roving information officers patrol on and around the promenade (on Segways!).

Hollywood

Dear sweet Hollywood, the vortex of a global entertainment industry, has some backstory. First, there was the Golden Age, the dawn of motion pictures, when industry strong-men ruled and owned it all. Then the '70s happened, which brought edgy productions even while studios fled in search of more space in Burbank and Studio City. Soon the only 'stars' left were embedded in the sidewalk. Worse, you had to hopscotch around runaways and addicts to see them. In the late '90s the momentum began to shift, and over the next 10 years, big, intelligent dollars, along with a touch of smart design, flooded the area and transformed it into what it is today. A gleaming, bustling, gritty, dazzling mosh pit of fun, food and questionable behavior.

⊙ Sights

Hollywood Bowl
Landmark

(www.hollywoodbowl.com; 2301 Highland Ave; rehearsals free, performance costs vary; ⊙ Apr-Sep; ℙ) Summers in LA wouldn't be the same without this chill spot for symphonies under the stars, and big-name acts from Baaba Maal and Sigur Rós to Radiohead and Paul McCartney. A huge natural amphitheater, the Hollywood Bowl has been around since 1922 and has great sound.

Hollywood Walk of Fame
Landmark

(www.walkoffame.com; Hollywood Blvd) Big Bird, Bob Hope, Marilyn Monroe and Aretha Franklin are among the stars being sought out, worshipped, photographed and stepped on along the Hollywood Walk of Fame. Since 1960 more than 2400 performers – from legends to bit-part players – have been honored with a pink-marble sidewalk star.

Grauman's Chinese Theatre
Landmark

(☎ 323-463-9576; www.tclchinesetheatres.com; 6925 Hollywood Blvd; tours & movie tickets adult/child/senior $13.50/6.50/11.50) Ever wondered what it's like to be in George Clooney's shoes? Just find his footprints in the forecourt of this world-famous movie palace. The exotic pagoda theater – complete with temple bells and stone heaven dogs from China – has shown movies since 1927 when Cecil B DeMille's *The King of Kings* first flickered across the screen.

Hollywood Sign
Landmark

LA's most famous landmark first appeared in the hills in 1923 as an advertising gimmick for a real-estate development called 'Hollywoodland'. Each letter is 50ft tall and made

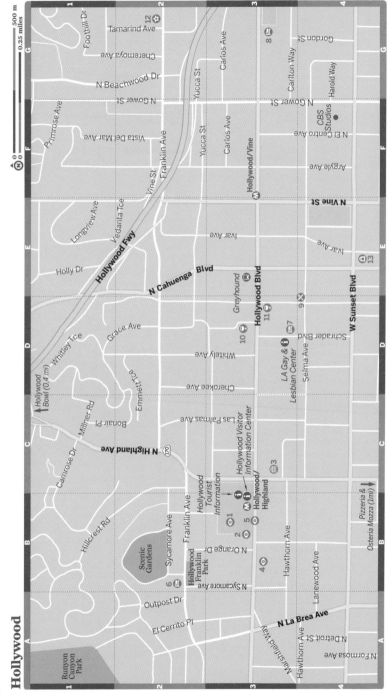

Hollywood

Hollywood

◎ Sights

1 Dolby Theatre...................... B3
2 Grauman's Chinese Theatre......... B3
3 Hollywood Museum C3
4 Hollywood Roosevelt Hotel.......... B3
5 Hollywood Walk of Fame B3

😎 Activities & Tours

TMZ Tours...................... see 2

🛏 Sleeping

6 Magic Castle Hotel B2
7 USA Hostels Hollywood D3
8 Vibe Hotel G3

✖ Eating

9 Little Fork D4

🍷 Drinking & Nightlife

10 Dirty Laundry..................... D3
    No Vacancy.................... see 10
11 Sayers Club....................... D3

⭐ Entertainment

12 Upright Citizens Brigade Theatre G2

🛍 Shopping

13 Amoeba Music E4

of sheet metal. Once aglow with 4000 light bulbs, the sign even had its own caretaker who lived behind the 'L' until 1939.

It's illegal to hike up to the sign, but viewing spots are plentiful, including Hollywood & Highland, the top of Beachwood Dr and the Griffith Observatory.

Hollywood Museum   Museum

(☑ 323-464-7776; www.thehollywoodmuseum.com; 1660 N Highland Ave; adult/child $15/5; ⊙10am-5pm Wed-Sun) We quite like this musty temple to the stars, crammed with kitsch posters, costumes and rotating props. The museum is housed inside the handsome 1914 art deco Max Factor Building, where the make-up pioneer once worked his magic on Hollywood stars such as Marilyn Monroe and Judy Garland.

Dolby Theatre   Theater

(www.dolbytheatre.com; 6801 Hollywood Blvd; tours adult/child, senior & student $17/12; ⊙10:30am-4pm) The Academy Awards are handed out at the Dolby Theatre, which has also hosted the *American Idol* finale, the ESPY awards,

the Miss USA pageant and a recent Neil Young residency. On the tour you get to sniff around the auditorium, admire a VIP room and see Oscar up close.

☞ Tours

TMZ Tours   Hollywood Tour

(☑ 855-4TMZ-TOUR; www.tmz.com/tour; 6925 Hollywood Blvd; adult/child $55/45; ⊙approx 10 tours daily) Cut the shame, do you really want to spot celebrities, glimpse their homes, and gawk and laugh at their dirt? Join this branded tour devised by paparazzi who have themselves become famous.

🛏 Sleeping

Vibe Hotel   Hostel $

(☑ 323-469-8600; www.vibehotel.com; 5920 Hollywood Blvd; dm $22-25, r $85-95; ℗@🛜) A funky motel-turned-hostel with both co-ed and female-only dorms – each with a flat screen and kitchenette – and several recently re-done private rooms that sleep three. You'll share space with a happening international crowd.

USA Hostels Hollywood   Hostel $

(☑ 800-524-6783, 323-462-3777; www.usahostels. com; 1624 Schrader Blvd; dm $30-40, r with shared bath $81-104; ❋@🛜) This sociable hostel puts you within steps of the Hollywood party circuit. Private rooms are a bit cramped, but making new friends is easy during staff-organized barbecues, comedy nights and $25 all-you-can-drink limo tours. Freebies include a cook-your-own-pancake breakfast. They have cushy lounge seating on the front porch and free beach shuttles.

Magic Castle Hotel   Hotel $$

(☑ 323-851-0800; http://magiccastlehotel. com; 7025 Franklin Ave; r incl breakfast from $174; ℗❋@🛜✖) Walls at this perennial pleaser are a bit thin, but otherwise it's a charming base of operation with large, modern rooms, exceptional staff and a petite courtyard pool where days start with fresh pastries and gourmet coffee. Enquire about access to the Magic Castle, a fabled members-only magic club in an adjacent Victorian mansion. Parking costs $10.

✕ Eating

Jitlada
Thai **$$**

(☑ 323-667-9809; jitladala.com; 5233 W Sunset Blvd; appetizers $5-10, mains $11-30; ⊘ lunch & dinner; Ⓟ) A transporting taste of southern Thailand. Its crab curry and fried *som tum* (papaya salad) are fantastic, as is its Thai-style burger. The vivacious owner operator counts Ryan Gosling and Natalie Portman among her loyal, mostly *farang* (European American) customers. Look for the wall of fame near the bathrooms.

Pikey
Pub **$$**

(☑ 323-850-5400; www.thepikeyla.com; 7617 W Sunset Blvd; dishes $12-28; ⊘ noon-2am Mon-Fri, from 11am Sat & Sun) A tasteful kitchen that began life as Coach & Horses, one of Hollywood's favorite dives before it was reimagined into a place where you can get broccoli roasted with bacon, Arctic char crudo with grapefruit and jalapenos, seared squid with curried chickpeas, and a slow-roasted duck leg. The cocktails rock.

Pizzeria & Osteria Mozza
Italian **$$$**

(☑ 323-297-0100; www.mozza-la.com; 6602 Melrose Ave; pizzas $11-19, dinner mains $27-38; ⊘ pizzeria noon-midnight daily, osteria 5:30-11pm Mon-Fri, 5-11pm Sat, 5-10pm Sun) Osteria Mozza is all about fine dining crafted from market fresh, seasonal ingredients, but being a Mario Batali joint you can expect adventure (think: squid-ink chitarra freddi with Dungeness crab, sea urchin and jalapeno) and consistent excellence. Reservations are recommended.

Little Fork
Southern **$$$**

(☑ 323-465-3675; www.littleforkla.com; 1600 Wilcox Ave; dishes $9-28; ⊘ 11am-3pm Sat & Sun, 5-10pm Sun-Thu, to midnight Fri & Sat; Ⓟ) The stucco exterior of this converted studio is a horror show, but inside all is dark and moody. More importantly, the kitchen churns out plates of house-smoked trout, brick-roasted chicken, potato gnocchi cooked in bacon lard, tarragon and cream, and a 1lb lobster roll!

☕ Drinking & Nightlife

La Descarga
Lounge

(☑ 323-466-1324; www.ladescargala.com; 1159 N Western Ave; ⊘ 8pm-2am Wed-Sat) This tastefully frayed, sublimely sweaty rum and cigar lounge is a revelation. Behind the marble bar there are more than 100 types of rum from Haiti and Guyana, Guatemala and Venezuela.

No Vacancy
Bar

(☑ 323-465-1902; www.novacancyla.com; 1727 N Hudson Ave; ⊘ 8pm-2am) An old, shingled Victorian has been converted into LA's hottest night out (at research time). Even the entrance is theatrical. You'll follow a rickety staircase into a narrow hall and enter the room of a would-be Madame (dressed in fishnet), who will press a button to reveal another staircase down into the living room and out into a courtyard of mayhem.

Dirty Laundry
Bar

(☑ 323-462-6531; dirtylaundrybarla.com; 1725 N Hudson Ave; ⊘ 10pm-2am) Under a cotton-candy-pink apartment block of no particular import is a funky den of musty odor and great times, low ceilings, exposed pipes, good whiskey, groovy funk on the turntables and plenty of uninhibited pretty people. There are velvet-rope politics at work here, so reserve a table to make sure you slip through.

Sayers Club
Club

(☑ 323-871-8416; www.sbe.com/nightlife/locations/thesayersclub-hollywood; 1645 Wilcox Ave; cover varies; ⊘ 8pm-2am Tue, Thu & Fri) When rock royalty such as Prince, established stars like the Black Keys and even movie stars like Joseph Gordon Levitt decide to play secret shows in intimate environs, they find the back room at this brick-house Hollywood nightspot, where the booths are leather, the lighting moody and the music – whether live, or spun by DJs – satisfies.

☆ Entertainment

Upright Citizens Brigade Theatre
Comedy

(☑ 323-908-8702; www.losangeles.ucbtheatre.com; 5919 Franklin Ave; tickets $5-10) Founded in New York by *SNL* alums Amy Poehler and Ian Roberts along with Matt Besser and Matt Walsh, this sketch-comedy group cloned itself in Hollywood in 2005 and is arguably the best improv theater in town. Most shows are $5 or $8, but Sunday's 'Asssscat' is freeeee.

🛍 Shopping

Amoeba Music
Music

(☑ 323-245-6400; www.amoeba.com; 6400 W Sunset Blvd; ⊘ 10:30am-11pm Mon-Sat, 11am-9pm Sun) When a record store not only survives but thrives in this techno age, you know it's doing something right. Flip through half-a-million new and used LPs, CDs, DVDs, videos and vinyl at this granddaddy of music stores. Handy listening stations and its outstanding *Music We Like* booklet keep you from buying lemons.

ℹ️ Information

Hollywood Visitor Information Center
(☑ 323-467-6412; http://discoverlosangeles.com; Hollywood & Highland complex, 6801 Hollywood Blvd, Hollywood; ⊙10am-10pm Mon-Sat, to 7pm Sun) In the Dolby Theatre walkway.

Pasadena

One could argue that there is more blue-blood, meat-eating, robust Americana in Pasadena than in all other LA neighborhoods combined. Here is a community with a preppy old soul, a historical perspective, an appreciation for art and jazz and a slightly progressive undercurrent.

The Rose Parade and Rose Bowl (☑ 626-577-3100; www.rosebowlstadium.com; 1001 Rose Bowl Dr) football game may have given Pasadena its long-lasting fame, but it's the spirit of this genteel city and its location beneath the lofty San Gabriel Mountains that make it a charming and attractive place year-round. Don't miss the Huntington Library (☑ 626-405-2100; www.huntington.org; 1151 Oxford Rd, San Marino; adult weekday/weekend & holidays $20/23, child $8, 1st Thu each month free; ⊙10:30am-4:30pm Wed-Mon Jun-Aug, noon-4:30pm Mon & Wed-Fri, from 10:30am Sat, Sun & holidays Sep-May; ℗), with it's tranquil Zen gardens, Norton Simon Museum (www.nortonsimon.org; 411 W Colorado Blvd; adult/child $10/free; ⊙noon-6pm Wed-Mon, to 9pm Fri; ℗), home to many a masterpiece, and when the Descanso Gardens (www.descansogardens.org; 1418 Descanso Dr, La Cañada Flintridge; adult/5-12yr/student & senior $9/4/6; ⊙9am-5pm; ℗) bloom in January and February, they're magic.

The two-lane Angeles Crest Scenic Byway (www.byways.org/explore/byways/10245/travel.html; Hwy 2) treats you to fabulous views of big-shouldered mountains, the Mojave Desert and deep valleys on its 55-mile meander from La Cañada to the resort town of Wrightwood. The road skirts LA County's tallest mountain, officially called Mt San Antonio (10,064ft), but better known as Old Baldy for its treeless top.

Huntington Library, Pasadena
BARRY WINIKER / GETTY IMAGES ©

🛏️ Sleeping

Bissell House B&B
B&B $$
(☑ 626-441-3535626-441-3535; www.bissellhouse.com; 201 S Orange Grove Blvd; r $159-259; ℗ 🛜 🏊) Antiques, hardwood floors and a crackling fireplace make this secluded Victorian B&B on 'Millionaire's Row' a bastion of warmth and romance. The hedge-framed garden feels like a sanctuary, and there's a pool for cooling off on hot days. The Prince Albert room has gorgeous wallpaper and a claw-foot tub. All seven rooms have private baths.

Langham
Resort $$$
(☑ 626-568-3900; www.pasadena.langhamhotels.com; 1401 S Oak Knoll Ave; r from $230; ℗ @ 🛜 🏊) Opened as the Huntington Hotel in 1906, this place spent the last several decades as the Ritz Carlton before recently donning the robes of Langham. But some things don't change: this incredible 23-acre, palm-dappled, beaux-arts country estate – complete with rambling gardens, giant swimming pool and covered picture bridge – has still got it. Rates are reasonable.

🍴 Eating

Little Flower
Cafe $
(☑ 626-304-4800; www.littleflowercandyco.com; 1424 W Colorado Blvd; mains $8-15; ⊙7am-7pm Mon-Sat, 9am-4pm Sun) Locally loved cafe set just a mile over the Colorado Bridge from

Old Town. It does exquisite pastries, *bánh mì* sandwiches with chicken, roast beef or tempeh, and bowls stuffed with such things as dahl, raita, curried eggplant and steamed spinach, or salmon, shredded carrots and daikon, micro greens and ponzu.

Los Angeles to Barstow

Heading out of the San Gabriel Valley, Colorado Pl turns into Huntington Dr E, which you'll follow to 2nd Ave, where you turn north, then east on Foothill Blvd. This older alignment of Route 66 follows Foothill Blvd through Monrovia, home of the 1925 Mayan Revival–style architecture of the allegedly haunted Aztec Hotel (☎626-358-3231; 311 W Foothill Blvd).

Continue east on W Foothill Blvd, then jog south on S Myrtle Ave and hook a left on E Huntington Dr through Duarte, which puts on a Route 66 parade (http://duarteroute66parade.com; ⊙September), with boisterous marching bands, old-fashioned carnival games and a classic-car show. In Azusa, Huntington turns into E Foothill Blvd, which becomes Alosta Blvd in Glendora where The Hat (☎626-857-0017; www.thehat.com; 611 W Route 66; mains $4-8; ⊙10am-11pm Sun-Wed, to 1am Thu-Sat; ⊕) has made piled-high pastrami sandwiches since 1951.

Continue east on Foothill Blvd, where two campily retro steakhouses await in Rancho Cucamonga. First up is the 1955 Magic Lamp Inn (☎909-981-8659; www.themagiclampinn.com; 8189 Foothill Blvd; mains lunch $11-17, dinner $15-42; ⊙11:30am-2:30pm Tue-Fri, 5-11pm Tue-Thu, 5-10:30pm Fri & Sat, 4-9pm Sun), easily recognized by its fabulous neon sign. There's dancing Wednesday through Saturday nights. Up the road, the rustic Sycamore Inn (☎909-982-1104; www.thesycamoreinn.com; 8318 Foothill Blvd, Rancho Cucamonga; mains $22-49; ⊙5-9pm Mon-Thu, to 10pm Fri & Sat, 4-8:30pm Sun) has been dishing up juicy steaks since 1848.

Foothill Blvd continues on to Rialto where you'll find the Wigwam Motel (☎909-875-3005; www.wigwammotel.com; 2728 W Foothill Blvd; r $65-80; ⊛), whose kooky concrete faux-tepees date from 1949. Continue east, then head north on N East St to the unofficial First McDonald's Museum (☎909-885-6324; 1398 N E St, San Bernardino; admission by donation; ⊙10am-5pm), which has interesting historic Route 66 exhibits. Continue north, then turn left on W Highland Ave and pick up the I-215 Fwy to I-15 and exit at Cleghorn for Cajon Blvd to

trundle north on an ancient section of the Mother Road. Get back onto I-15 and drive up to the Cajon Pass. At the top, take the Oak Hill Rd exit (No 138) to the Summit Inn Cafe (☎760-949-8688; 5960 Mariposa Rd, Hesperia; mains $5-10; ⊙6am-8pm Mon-Thu, to 9pm Fri & Sat), a 1950s roadside diner with antique gas pumps, a retro jukebox and a lunch counter that serves ostrich burgers and date shakes.

Get back on I-15 and drive downhill to Victorville, exiting at 7th St and driving past the San Bernardino County Fairgrounds, home of the Route 66 Raceway. Along 7th St in Old Town Victorville, look for landmarks including the bucking bronco sign of the New Corral Motel. At D St, turn left for the excellent California Route 66 Museum (☎760-951-0436; www.califrt66museum.org; 16825 D St; donations welcome; ⊙10am-4pm Thu-Sat & Mon, 11am-3pm Sun), opposite the Greyhound bus station. Inside a former cafe is a wonderfully eclectic collection including a 1930s teardrop trailer, sparkling red naughahyde booth with tabletop mini-jukebox, advertising signage, vintage photos, and bits and pieces from the Roy Rogers Museum that used to be in Victorville before moving to Branson, Missouri (where it closed in 2010).

In Oro Grande, the Iron Hog Saloon (20848 National Trails Hwy; ⊙8am-10pm Mon-Thu & Sun, to 2am Fri & Sat) is an old-time honky-tonk dripping with memorabilia and character(s). It's hugely popular with bikers and serves large portions of rib-stickers, including rattlesnake and ostrich. About 5 miles further north, Bottle Tree Ranch (Elmer's Place; 24266 National Trails Hwy) is a colorful roadside folk-art collection of glass bottles artfully arranged on telephone poles along with weathered railroad signs.

Barstow

At the junction of I-40 and I-15, nearly halfway between LA and Las Vegas, down-and-out Barstow (population 23,000) has been a desert travelers' crossroads for centuries. In 1776 Spanish colonial priest Francisco Garcés caravanned through, and in the mid-19th century the Old Spanish Trail passed nearby, with pioneer settlers on the Mojave River selling supplies to California immigrants. Meanwhile, mines were founded in the hills outside town. Barstow, named after a railway executive, got going as a railroad junction after 1886. After 1926 it became a major rest stop for motorists along Route 66 (Main St). Today it exists to serve nearby military bases and is still a busy pit stop for travelers.

⊙ Sights

Barstow is well known for its history-themed murals that spruce up often empty and boarded-up downtown buildings, mostly along Main St between 1st and 6th Sts. Pick up a map at the Chamber of Commerce.

Route 66 'Mother Road' Museum Museum
(☎760-255-1890; www.route66museum.org; 681 N 1st St; ⊙10am-4pm Fri & Sat, 11am-4pm Sun, or by appointment) FREE Inside the beautifully restored Casa del Desierto, a 1911 Harvey House (architecturally significant railway inns named for their originator Fred Harvey), this museum documents life along the historic highway with some great old black-and-white photographs alongside eclectic relics, including a 1915 Ford Model T, a 1913 telephone switchboard and products made from locally mined minerals. The excellent gift shop stocks Route 66 driving guides, maps and books.

Desert Discovery Center Museum
(☎760-252-6060; www.desertdiscoverycenter.com; 831 Barstow Rd; ⊙11am-4pm Tue-Sat; ⊕) FREE The US Bureau of Land Management operates this kid-oriented, educational center in an adobe building near I-15. Activities include animal-feeding, art club and monthly programs from drums to composting, and you can get info on exploring the local deserts. The star exhibit is the Old Woman Meteorite, the second-largest ever found in the USA, weighing in at a hefty 6070lbs.

Calico Ghost Town Theme Park
See p42. See p42.

🛏 Sleeping & Eating

Only when the Mojave freezes over will there be no rooms left in Barstow. Just drive along E Main St and take your pick from the string of national chain motels, many with doubles from $40.

Oak Tree Inn Motel $
(☎760-254-1148; www.oaktreeinn.com; 35450 Yermo Rd, Yermo; r incl breakfast $53-74; P❄⚡☀☕) For class and comfort, steer towards this three-story, 65-room motel near the freeway, where rooms have black-out draperies and triple-paned windows. It's 11 miles east of town (exit Ghost Town Rd off I-15). Breakfast is served at the adjacent 1950s-style diner.

Lola's Kitchen Mexican $
(1244 E Main St; mains $5-12; ⊙4am-7:30pm Mon-Fri, to 4:30pm Sat; ⊕) Interstate truckers, blue-collar workers and Vegas-bound hipsters all gather at this simple, colorful Mexican *cocina,* tucked away inside a strip mall and run by two sisters who make succulent *carne asada* burritos, *chile verde* enchiladas and more.

Idle Spurs Steakhouse Steakhouse $$
(☎760-256-8888; www.idlespurssteakhouse.com; 690 Hwy 58; mains lunch $10-24, dinner $14-28; ⊙11am-9pm Mon-Fri, from 4pm Sat & Sun; ⊕) In the saddle since 1950, this Western-themed spot, ringed around an atrium and a full bar, is a fave with locals and RVers. Surrender to your inner carnivore with slow-roasted prime rib, hand-cut steaks and succulent lobster tail. Kids menu available. It's a couple miles off Rte 66.

Peggy Sue's Diner $$
(☎760-254-3370; www.peggysuesdiner.com; Ghost Town Rd, Yermo; mains $8-13; ⊙6am-10pm; ⊕) Built in 1954 as a simple, nine-stool, three-booth diner, Peggy Sue's has since grown into a mini-empire with ice-cream shop, pizza parlor, a park out back with metal sculptures of 'diner-saurs' and a kitschy-awesome gift shop. It's down the street from Oak Tree Inn.

☆ Entertainment

Skyline Drive-In Cinema
(☎760-256-3333; 31175 Old Hwy 58; adult/child $7/2; ⊕) One of the few drive-ins left in California, this 1960s movie theater shows one or two flicks nightly.

ⓘ Information

Barstow Area Chamber of Commerce
(☎760-256-8617; www.barstowchamber.com; 681 N 1st Ave; ⊙8:30am-5:30pm Mon-Fri, 10am-2pm Sat; 🤙) At the train station, just north of downtown.

Barstow to Needles

Leave Barstow on I-40 east and exit at Daggett (exit 7), site of the California inspection station once dreaded by Dust Bowl refugees. Drive north on A St, cross the railroad tracks and turn right on Santa Fe St. On your left, just past the general store, you'll see the moodily

Crumbling houses, Needles

crumbling, late-19th-century Daggett Stone Hotel, where desert adventurers such as Death Valley Scotty used to stay.

Continue on Santa Fe, take your first right, then turn left to pick up the National Trails Hwy going east.

Shortly after the highway ducks under I-40, you're in Newberry Springs, where the grizzled, 1950s Bagdad Cafe (☑ 760-257-3101; www.bagdadcafethereal.com; 46548 National Trails Hwy; mains $6-12; ☺ 7am-7pm) was the main filming location of the eponymous 1987 indie flick starring CCH Pounder and Jack Palance, a cult hit in Europe. The interior is chockablock with posters, movie stills and momentos left by fans, while outside, the old water tower and airstream trailer are slowly rusting away.

The National Trails Hwy runs south along the freeway, crosses it at Lavic and continues east along the northern side of I-40. This potholed, crumbling backcountry stretch of Route 66 crawls through ghostly desert towns. In Ludlow turn right on Crucero Rd, cross I-40 again and pick up the highway by turning left.

Beyond Ludlow, Route 66 veers away from the freeway and bumps along past haunting ruins spliced into the majestic landscape. Only a few landmarks interrupt the limitless horizon, most famously the sign of the well-preserved but defunct, 1950s Roy's Motel & Cafe (there's a working gas station and small shop). It's east of Amboy Crater, an almost perfectly symmetrical volcanic cinder cone that went dormant 600 years ago. You can scramble up its west side (don't attempt it in high winds or summer heat).

Past Essex the Mother Road leaves National Trails Hwy and heads north on Goffs Rd through Fenner, where it once more crosses I-40. In Goffs the one-room, 1914 Mission-style Goffs Schoolhouse (☑ 760-733-4482; www.mdhca.org; 37198 Lanfair Rd; donations welcome; ☺ usually 9am-4pm Sat & Sun) remains part of the best-preserved historic settlement in the Mojave Desert.

Continue on Goffs Rd (US Hwy 95) to I-40 East and follow it to Needles. Named after nearby mountain spires, it's the last Route 66 stop before the Arizona border, where the Old Trails Arch Bridge carried the Joad family across the Colorado River in *The Grapes of Wrath*.

Exit at J St and turn left, follow J St to W Broadway, turn right and then left on F St, which runs into Front St, paralleling the railway track. Go past the old mule-train wagon and 1920s Palm Motel to El Garces, a 1908 Harvey House that's been undergoing restorations for years.

USA Driving Guide

With a comprehensive network of interstate highways, enthusiastic car culture and jaw-dropping scenery, the USA is an ideal road-tripping destination.

DRIVER'S LICENSE & DOCUMENTS

All US drivers must carry a valid driving license from their home state, proof of vehicle insurance and their vehicle's registration papers or a copy of their vehicle-rental contract.

Foreign drivers can legally drive in the USA for 12 months using their home driver's license. An International Driving Permit (IDP) isn't required, but will have more credibility with traffic police and will simplify the car-rental process, especially if your home license isn't written in English and/or doesn't have a photo. International automobile associations issue IDPs, valid for one year, for a fee. Always carry your home license with your IDP.

The American Automobile Association (AAA) has reciprocal agreements with some international auto clubs (eg Canada's CAA, AA in the UK). Bring your membership card from home.

INSURANCE

Liability insurance is legally required for all vehicles, although minimum coverage varies by state. When renting a car, check your home auto-insurance policy and, if applicable, your travel-insurance policy to see if rental cars are already covered. If not, expect to pay about $15 a day for rental-car liability insurance.

Insurance against damage to the car, called Collision Damage Waiver (CDW) or Loss Damage Waiver (LDW), adds another $15 to $20 per day for rental cars. Even with a CDW/LDW, you may be required to

pay up to the first $500 for any repairs. If you decline CDW/LDW, you will be held liable for damages up to the car's full value.

Some credit cards cover CDW/LDW if you charge the entire cost of the car rental to that card. If you have an accident, you may be required to pay the car-rental company first, then seek reimbursement from the credit-card issuer. Most credit-card coverage isn't valid for rentals over 15 days or 'exotic' models (eg convertibles, 4WD Jeeps).

RENTING A VEHICLE

To rent your own wheels, you'll usually need to be at least 25 years old, hold a valid driver's license and have a major credit card, *not* a check or debit card.

Cars

Rental car rates generally include unlimited mileage, but expect surcharges for additional drivers and one-way rentals.

Driving Fast Facts

➡ **Right or left?** Drive on the right
➡ **Legal driving age** 16
➡ **Top speed limit** 70mph on some highways.
➡ **Best bumper sticker** 'Where the heck is Wall Drug?'
➡ **Best radio station** National Public Radio (NPR)

Road Trip Websites

AUTO CLUBS

American Automobile Association (www.aaa.com) Roadside assistance, travel discounts, trip planning and maps for members.

Better World Club (www.betterworldclub.com) Ecofriendly alternative to AAA.

MAPS

America's Byways (http://byways.org) Inspiring itineraries, maps and directions for scenic drives.

Google Maps (http://maps.google.com) Turn-by-turn driving directions with estimated traffic delays.

ROAD CONDITIONS & CLOSURES

US Department of Transportation (www.fhwa.dot.gov/trafficinfo) Links to state and local road conditions, traffic and weather.

Airport locations may have cheaper base rates but higher add-on fees. If you get a fly-drive package, local taxes may be extra when you pick up the car. Child and infant safety seats are legally required; reserve them (around $10 per day, or $50 per trip) when booking your car.

Some major car-rental companies offer 'green' fleets of hybrid or alternative-fuel rental cars, but they're in short supply. Make reservations far in advance and expect to pay significantly more for these models. Many companies rent vans with wheelchair lifts and hand-controlled vehicles at no extra cost, but you must also reserve these well in advance.

International car-rental companies with hundreds of branches nationwide include:

Alamo (www.alamo.com)

Avis (www.avis.com)

Budget (www.budget.com)

Dollar (www.dollar.com)

Enterprise (www.enterprise.com)

Fox (www.foxrentacar.com)

Hertz (www.hertz.com)

National (www.nationalcar.com)

Thrifty (www.thrifty.com)

To find local and independent car-rental companies, check:

Car Rental Express (www.carrentalexpress.com) Search for independent car-rental companies and specialty cars (eg hybrids).

Rent-a-Wreck (www.rentawreck.com) Often rents to younger drivers (over-18s) and those without credit cards; ask about long-term rentals.

Wheelchair Getaways (www.wheelchairgetaways.com) Rents wheelchair-accessible vans across the country.

Zipcar (www.zipcar.com) Car-sharing club in dozens of cities; some foreign drivers are eligible for membership.

If you don't mind no-cancellation policies or which company you rent from, you may find better deals on car rentals through online travel discounters such as **Priceline** (www.priceline.com) and **Hotwire** (www.hotwire.com).

Motorcycles

Motorcycle rentals and insurance are very expensive, with steep surcharges for one-way rentals. Discounts may be available for three-day and weekly rentals.

National rental outfitters include:

Eagle Rider (www.eaglerider.com) Motorcycle rentals and tours in more than 25 states.

Harley-Davidson (www.harley-davidson.com) Links to scores of local motorcycle shops that rent Harleys.

RVs & Campervans

Popular with road-trippers, recreational vehicles (RVs, also called motorhomes) are cumbersome to drive and burn fuel at an alarming rate. However, they do solve transportation, accommodation and self-catering kitchen needs in one fell swoop. Even so, there are many places in national parks and scenic areas (eg narrow mountain roads) that they can't be driven.

Make reservations for RVs and smaller campervans as far in advance as possible. Rental costs vary by size and model; basic rates often don't include mileage, bedding or kitchen kits, vehicle prep and cleaning or additional taxes and fees. If bringing pets is allowed, a surcharge may apply.

National rental agencies include:

Cruise America (www.cruiseamerica.com) With 125 RV rental locations nationwide.

El Monte RV (www.elmonterv.com) RV rentals in more than 25 states.

Happy Travel Campers (www.camperusa. com) Rents campervans in Los Angeles, San Francisco, Las Vegas and Denver.

Jucy Rentals (www.jucyrentals.com) Campervan rentals in Los Angeles, San Francisco and Las Vegas.

BORDER CROSSING

Citizens of Canada and Mexico who are driving across the border should be sure to bring their vehicle's registration papers, proof of liability insurance valid for driving in the USA and their home driving license. An International Driving Permit (IDP) isn't required, but may be helpful. Only some rental-car companies allow their vehicles to be driven across international borders.

Drunk Driving

The maximum legal blood-alcohol concentration for drivers is 0.08%. Penalties for 'DUI' (driving under the influence of alcohol or drugs) are severe, including heavy fines, driver's license suspension, court appearances and/or jail time. Police may give roadside sobriety checks to assess if you've been drinking or using drugs. If you fail, they'll require you to take a breath, urine or blood test to determine the level of drugs and alcohol in your body. Refusing to be tested is treated the same as if you'd taken the test and failed.

USA Playlist

(Get Your Kicks on) Route 66 Bobby Troup, as recorded by Nat King Cole

I've Been Everywhere Johnny Cash

This Land Is Your Land Woody Guthrie

Born to Be Wild Steppenwolf

Runnin' Down a Dream Tom Petty & the Heartbreakers

Life Is a Highway Tom Cochrane

MAPS

Tourist information offices and visitor centers distribute free but often very basic maps. GPS navigation can't be relied upon everywhere, notably in thick forests and remote mountain, desert and canyon areas. If you're planning on doing a lot of driving, you may want a more detailed fold-out road map or map atlas, such as those published by **Rand McNally** (www. randmcnally.com). Members of the American Automobile Association (AAA) and its international auto-club affiliates (bring your membership card from home) can pick up free maps at AAA branch offices nationwide.

ROADS & CONDITIONS

The USA's highways are not always perfect ribbons of unblemished asphalt. Common road hazards include potholes, rockfalls, mudslides, flooding, fog, free-ranging livestock and wildlife, commuter traffic jams on weekday mornings and afternoons, and drivers distracted by technology, kids and pets or blinded by road rage.

In places where winter driving is an issue, snow tires and tire chains may be necessary, especially in the mountains. Ideally, carry your own chains and learn how to use them before you hit the road. Driving off-road or on dirt roads is often forbidden by rental-car contracts, and it can be very dangerous in wet weather.

Major highways, expressways and bridges in some urban areas require paying tolls. Sometimes tolls can be paid using cash (bills or coins), but occasionally an electronic toll-payment sensor

Driving Problem-Buster

What should I do if my car breaks down? Put on your hazard lights (flashers) and carefully pull over to the side of the road. Call the roadside emergency assistance number for your auto club or rental-car company. Otherwise, call information (☑411) for the number of the nearest towing service or auto-repair shop.

What if I have an accident? If you're safely able to do so, move your vehicle out of traffic and onto the road's shoulder. For minor collisions with no major property damage or bodily injuries, be sure to exchange driver's license and auto-insurance information with the other driver, then file a report with your insurance provider or notify your car-rental company as soon as possible. For major accidents, call ☑911 and wait for the police and emergency services to arrive.

What should I do if I'm stopped by the police? Don't get out of the car unless asked. Keep your hands where the officer can see them (ie on the steering wheel). Always be courteous. Most fines for traffic or parking violations can be handled by mail or online within a 30-day period.

What happens if my car gets towed? Call the local non-emergency police number and ask where to pick up your car. Towing and vehicle storage fees accumulate quickly, up to hundreds of dollars for just a few hours or a day, so act promptly.

is required. If you don't have one, your vehicle's license plate will likely be photographed and you'll be billed later, usually at a higher rate. Ask about this when picking up your rental vehicle to avoid surprising surcharges on your final bill after you've returned the car.

ROAD RULES

➡ Drive on the right-hand side of the road.

➡ Talking or texting on a cell (mobile) phone while driving is illegal in most states.

➡ The use of seat belts and infant and child safety seats is legally required nationwide, although exact regulations vary by state.

➡ Wearing motorcycle helmets is mandatory in many states, and always a good idea.

➡ High-occupancy vehicle (HOV) lanes marked with a diamond symbol are reserved for cars with multiple occupants, but sometimes only during specific signposted hours.

➡ Unless otherwise posted, the speed limit is generally 55mph or 65mph on highways, 25mph to 35mph in cities and towns and as low as 15mph in school zones. It's illegal to pass a school bus when its lights are flashing.

➡ Except where signs prohibit doing so, turning right at a red light after coming to a full stop is usually permitted (one notable exception is New York City). Intersecting cross-traffic still has the right of way, however.

➡ At four-way stop signs, cars proceed in order of arrival. If two cars arrive simultaneously, the one on the right goes first. When in doubt, politely wave the other driver ahead.

➡ At intersections, U-turns may be legal unless otherwise posted, but this varies by state – don't do it in Illinois, for example.

➡ When emergency vehicles approach from either direction, carefully pull over to the side of the road.

➡ In many states, it's illegal to carry open containers of alcohol (even if they're empty) inside a vehicle. Unless the containers are full and still sealed, put them in the trunk instead.

➡ Most states have strict anti-littering laws; throwing trash from a vehicle may incur a $1000 fine. Besides, it's bad for the environment.

➡ Hitchhiking is illegal in some states, and restricted in others.

PARKING

Free parking is plentiful in small towns and rural areas, but scarce and often expensive in cities. Municipal parking meters and centralized pay stations usually accept coins and credit or debit cards. Parking at broken meters is often prohibited; where allowed, the posted time limit still applies.

When parking on the street, carefully read all posted regulations and restrictions (eg 30-minute maximum, no parking during scheduled street-cleaning hours) and pay attention to colored curbs, or you may be ticketed and towed. In many towns and cities, overnight street parking is prohibited downtown and in designated areas reserved for local residents with permits.

At city parking garages and lots, expect to pay at least $2 per hour and $10 to $45 for all-day or overnight parking. For valet parking at hotels, restaurants, nightclubs etc, a flat fee of $5 to $40 is typically charged. Tip the valet attendant at least $2 when your keys are handed back to you.

FUEL

Gas stations are everywhere, except in national parks, rural areas and remote regions (eg mountains, deserts). Most gas stations are self-service.

Gas is sold in gallons (one US gallon equals 3.78L). The average price for regular-grade gas averages $3.15 to $4.25 across the country.

SAFETY

Vehicle theft, break-ins and vandalism are a problem mostly in urban areas. Be sure to lock your vehicle's doors, leave the windows rolled up and use any anti-theft devices that have been installed (eg car alarm, steering-wheel lock). Do not leave any valuables visible inside your vehicle; instead, stow them in the trunk before arriving at your destination, or else take them with you once you've parked.

BEHIND THE SCENES

ACKNOWLEDGMENTS

Climate map data adapted from Peel MC, Finlayson BL & McMahon TA (2007) 'Updated World Map of the Köppen-Geiger Climate Classification', *Hydrology and Earth System Sciences*, 11, 163344.

Cover photographs: Front: 1957 Ford T-Bird on Route 66 in Laguna, New Mexico, Car Culture/ Getty; Back: Santa Monica Pier, Verity E. Mulligan/ Getty.

THIS BOOK

This 1st edition of *Route 66 Road Trips* was researched and written by Karla Zimmerman, Amy Balfour and Nate Cavalieri. This guidebook was produced by the following:

Product Editor Katie O'Connell

Senior Cartographer Alison Lyall

Book Designer Katherine Marsh

Assisting Editors Melanie Dankel, Kirsten Rawlings

Assisting Book Designer Cam Ashley

Cover Researchers Brendan Dempsey, Campbell McKenzie

Thanks to Shahara Ahmed, Sasha Baskett, James Hardy, Kate James, Darren O'Connell, Martine Power, Angela Tinson, Dora Whitaker

OUR STORY

A beat-up old car, a few dollars in the pocket and a sense of adventure. In 1972 that's all Tony and Maureen Wheeler needed for the trip of a lifetime – across Europe and Asia overland to Australia. It took several months, and at the end – broke but inspired – they sat at their kitchen table writing and stapling together their first travel guide, *Across Asia on the Cheap*. Within a week they'd sold 1500 copies. Lonely Planet was born.

Today, Lonely Planet has offices in Melbourne, London and Oakland, with more than 600 staff and writers. We share Tony's belief that 'a great guidebook should do three things: inform, educate and amuse'.

INDEX

A

accommodations 13, *see also individual locations*
airports 13
Albuquerque 31, 73-9, **74**
Amarillo 30
Amboy 41-2
aquariums 46, 51, 75
Arcadia 43
Arizona 90-9
art 31, *see also* galleries, museums
Atlanta 20
Aztec Hotel 46

B

Barstow 42, 108-9
Blue Hole 72
books 36
border crossings 113
budgeting 13
business hours 13

C

Cadillac Ranch 30
Calico Ghost Town 42, **44-5**
California, *see* Western Route 66
campervan rental 112-13

000 Map pages
000 Photo pages

Canyon Road 87
car insurance 111
car rental 12, 111-12
cars, *see* driving
cell phones 12
Central Route 66 27-37, 70-99, **27**, **28-9**
Chicago 10, 18-19, 50-9, **52-3**, **10**, **51**, **59**
climate 12
costs 13

D

Daggett 42
driving
  campervan rental 112-13
  car rental 12, 111-12
  documents 111
  driver's license 111
  driving under the influence 113
  fuel 12, 115
  insurance 111
  maps 113
  motorcycle rental 112
  parking 114-15
  road rules 114
  Route 66 42
  RV rental 112-13
  safety 113
  tolls 113-14
  websites 112
Duarte 43, 108

E

Eastern Route 66 17-25, 50-68, **17**, **18-9**
El Reno 24
Elena Gallegos Open Space 75-6
Elmer's Place 42-3
emergencies 12

F

Flagstaff 34, 92-6, **93**
Fontana 43
food 13, *see also individual locations*
fuel 12, 115

G

galleries 87, *see also* museums
Gallup 31, 89-90, **48-9**
gas 12, 115
Gemini Giant 19-20, **16**
Glendora 108
Goffs 41, 110
Golden Shores 99
Grand Canyon Caverns 35, 97
Grapes of Wrath, The 35, 36, 41, 42, 110
Grauman's Chinese Theatre 103
Guthrie, Woody 23, 36, 66

H

Hackberry 35, 97, **32**
Havasu National Wildlife
  Refuge 99
Hesperia 43
hiking
  Albuquerque 75-6
  Flagstaff 94
  Gallup 89
  Santa Fe 81
history 35
Holbrook 91, **14-15**
Hollywood 45-6, 103-7, **104**
Hollywood Bowl 103
Hollywood Sign 103
Hollywood Walk of Fame 103
Homolovi State Park 91
Hualapai Mountain Park 98
Humphreys Peak 94

I

Illinois 50-60
insurance 111
internet access 12

K

Kachina Point 91
Kansas 21, 65
Kingman 35-6, 97-9, **32**, **33**

L

La Cieneguilla Petroglyph
  Site 81
Lebanon 9, 21, **9**
Lincoln, Abraham 20
literature 36
Los Angeles 11, 43-6, 100-10,
  102, **104**, **9**, **11**, **47**, **101**
Los Angeles International
  Airport 13

M

maps 113
McLean 29
Meteor Crater 33-4
Missouri 60-5
mobile phones 12
money 13
motorcycle rental 112
motorhome rental 112-13
museums
  Albuquerque Museum of
    Art & History 75
  American International
    Rattlesnake Museum 75
  Field Museum of Natural
    History 51
  Georgia O'Keeffe
    Museum 80-1
  Hollywood Museum 105
  Indian Pueblo Cultural
    Center 75
  Mesalands Dinosaur
    Museum 30
  Mohave Museum of History
    & Arts 98
  Museum of Indian Arts &
    Culture 81
  Museum of International
    Folk Art 80-1
  Museum of Northern
    Arizona 92-3
  New Mexico Museum
    of Natural History &
    Science 75
  Oklahoma City National
    Memorial Museum 24
  Oklahoma Route 66
    Museum 24
  Route 66 Auto Museum 72
  Route 66 'Mother Road'
    Museum (Barstow) 109
  Route 66 Museum
    (Kingsman) 36
music 113

N

Needles 41, 110, **110**
Newberry Springs 42
New Mexico 70-99

O

Oatman 36, 99
O'Hare International Airport
  Chicago 13
O'Keeffe, Georgia 80
Oklahoma 65-8
Oklahoma City 23-4, 67-8,
  66, **69**
Old Chain of Rocks Bridge 21
opening hours 13

P

Painted Desert 91
Palisades Park 46
parking 114-15
  Chicago 10
  Los Angeles 11
Pasadena 43, 45, 107-8, **107**
Petrified Forest National
  Park 31, 33-4, 90-1
petroglyphs
  Homolovi State Park 91
  La Cieneguilla Petroglyph
    Site 81
  Petroglyph National
    Monument 75
petrol 12, 115
photography 17, 27, 39
Puerto de Luna 72
Pyramid Rock 89

R

Raven's Ridge 81
Red Rock Park 89
rental cars 12, 111-12
Riordan Mansion State
  Historic Park 34

road rules 114
road tolls 113-14
RV rental 112-13

S

safety 70, 113
San Bernardino 43, 108
Sandia Crest 76
Santa Fe 30, 79-88, **82-3**, **79**, **85**
Santa Monica 9, 46-7, 100-3, **102**, **9**, **47**, **101**
Santa Monica Pier 46, 100, **101**
Santa Rosa 72-3

Seligman 34-5, 97, **96**
Sitgreaves Pass 99
Snow Cap Drive-In 35
Springfield 20, 59-60
St Louis 20, 60-5, **61**, **62**
Steinbeck, John 35, 36

T

telephone services 12
Tent Rocks 81
Texas 70
tipping 13
Topock Gorge 99
Tucumcari 9, 30-1, 71-2, **9**, **71**
Tulsa 22-3, 65-7, **64**

V

Venice 100-3, **102**, **11**
Victorville 43, 108

W

Walnut Canyon National Monument 92
weather 12, 17, 27, 39
websites 10, 11, 13
Western Route 66 39-47, 100-10, **39**, **40-1**
wi-fi 12
Winslow 33, 91-2

OUR WRITERS

KARLA ZIMMERMAN

Karla is a life-long Midwesterner, well-versed in the region's beaches, ballparks, breweries and pie shops. When she's not home in Chicago watching the Cubs (or writing for magazines, websites and books), she's exploring. Karla has written for several Lonely Planet guides to the USA, Canada, the Caribbean and Europe.

AMY BALFOUR

Amy has authored or co-authored more than 15 books for Lonely Planet and has written for *Backpacker*, *Every Day with Rachael Ray*, *Redbook*, *Southern Living* and *Women's Health*.

NATE CAVALIERI

Born and raised in rural Michigan, Nate Cavalieri authors guides for Lonely Planet on the US, Central America and the Caribbean, writes about music and maintains several fictional twitter accounts about professional cycling. He lives in Oakland. Look him up at www.natecavalieri.com.

← MORE WRITERS

Published by Lonely Planet Publications Pty Ltd
ABN 36 005 607 983
1st edition – May 2015
ISBN 978 1 74360 706 0
© Lonely Planet 2015   Photographs © as indicated 2015
10 9 8 7 6 5 4 3 2 1
Printed in China

Although the authors and Lonely Planet have taken all reasonable care in preparing this book, we make no warranty about the accuracy or completeness of its content and, to the maximum extent permitted, disclaim all liability arising from its use.